APR 2 1974

Archbishop Mitty High School
Library
5000 Mitty Avenue
San Jose, California

RULES

1. Books may be kept two weeks and may be renewed (ARCHBISHOP MITTY LIBRARY   day books
and ma

2. A   ed on each
book wh   above rule.
No bool   558   ng such a
fine unt..

3. All injuries to books, beyond reasonable wear, and
all losses shall be made good to the satisfaction of the
Librarian.

4. Each borrower is held responsible for all books
drawn on his card and for all fines accruing on the same.

3M 11-29-67

SLAVERY DEFENDED:

the views of
THE OLD SOUTH.

EDITED BY:

ERIC L. McKITRICK,

Associate Professor of History

at

COLUMBIA UNIVERSITY.

A SPECTRUM BOOK
published by
PRENTICE-HALL, Incorporated
ENGLEWOOD CLIFFS, NEW JERSEY

Printed in the United States of America

81280-C

For My Parents,

COLLEEN and FRED McKITRICK.

CONTENTS

THE DEFENSE OF SLAVERY

BY ERIC L. McKITRICK.

NOTHING IS MORE SUSCEPTIBLE to oblivion than an argument, however ingenious, that has been discredited by events; and such is the case with the body of writing which was produced in the antebellum South in defense of Negro slavery. In the one hundred years since emancipation, almost the whole of that work has remained superbly unread. What we know about the pro-slavery intellectuals and their writings is known not directly but through tag-names and hearsay. History books refer to them, but with a flicker of impatience, having little time to spend on crackpots.

To some extent, of course, this is an exaggeration. There have been exceptions to this general neglect, exceptions which provide a certain counterpoint of irony. Portions of George Fitzhugh's writings have recently been reprinted, and for some years the political and social thought of John C. Calhoun has been an object of recurrent interest. And yet that interest has centered not so much upon these thinkers' concern for preserving slavery as upon their critique of Northern and European capitalism. Their understanding of socialism, their perception of class conflict, the labor theory of value which they developed, their attacks on "wage slavery" and the mindless exploitations of industrialism—all of which anticipated Marx—have won for them a certain grudging attention.

But Calhoun and Fitzhugh were not the only ones to expound these ideas. Surveying the literature as a whole, one is surprised to find how generally such notions were shared in the intellectual South and how variously the "wage slave" theme found its way into the discourse. The effort attracted a considerable range of talents, temperaments, and ingenuity, and this in itself should promise that a fresh sampling might yield a few unsuspected discoveries.

There are other themes as well. The Southern thinkers drew much from the notions of Aristotle on order and function in society. They examined Scripture: their Bible argument is really something more than an exercise in equivocation; it is strong historical exegesis, and on this plane the Southern divines had clearly the better of their Northern counterparts. There was the "King Cotton" theory, which showed how the iron necessities of world trade upheld slavery. The Southerners also appealed to Burke, as they tried to predict the pernicious consequences of emancipation. They even had recourse to science, a science that was not merely Southern; theories of racial inferiority were not to be wholly discredited until well into the twentieth century. And in a purely literary vein, they achieved a lyricism which was by no means all counterfeit as they depicted the genial side of plantation life. All of these versions of the pro-slavery argument are represented in the present volume. Their exponents were not obscure men; all were known for their writings throughout the literate South; each exercised, for a time, wide influence.

The main moral issue of the debate has long since been settled. But the pro-slavery argument, whatever its perversity, is intrinsically more interesting than that of the abolitionists because it is more difficult and more complex. And the Southern critique of industrialism can make more than a passing claim to social analysis. In a society which, prior to the middle 1830s, did not seem to be fostering any serious dialectic as to its own basic values, the attacks of the abolitionists forced these men to think about first principles. The artificial "feudalism" which they postulated for themselves did, at least, allow them certain perceptions into the character of liberal society.

II

If one result, then, of a serious challenge to a set of social arrangements is to call forth a great deal of intellectual agility, as with the thinkers of the ante-bellum South, this is not the only thing that happens under such conditions. The intellectual conse-

quences of a challenge to institutions—and of the discipline needed
to defend them—are not all salutary. A further aspect of pro-slavery
thought, still leaving aside the rightness or wrongness of slavery,
is its essential arrogance. Its social thinking is barren simply because true richness is the one thing it cannot afford; the setting in
which it took place guaranteed that a critical analysis of slavery
itself, even the most benevolent and constructive, was by that time
out of the question. A previous generation of Southern intellectuals
—that of Jefferson and Madison—wrestled with problems of liberty
and government, but they tended to do so in rather an *ad hoc* way
as circumstances required; intellectually the results were disor-
ganized and somewhat blurred. Not so with the pro-slavery thinkers.
These men had orthodoxy all laid out for them and were develop-
ing it with all the ingenuity they could muster. This is what enabled them to be such elegant system-makers; even the "originality"
of a Calhoun is placed in some doubt when we discover the extent
to which his principal dogmas were the currency of his time.

The quasi-Marxist content of pro-slavery thought has attracted
the attention of several modern writers, but the "Marxist" comparison need not be limited simply to content. There is an analogy
also to be found in the style of mind. Among the most striking
qualities of Marxist social thought is its inability to analyze itself.
Decisions are taken in Marxist countries by men who have power,
while the intellectuals explain and justify them by manipulating
symbols. Since the relationship between power and intellect in such
a culture is for the most part rigid and brittle, the Marxist intellectual, held to the mark at home, does not become really effective
until he is dealing with outside societies. In such cases he can occasionally arrive at flashing insights. But within his own system
his one great imperative is orthodoxy. Receptivity and responsive-
ness, true speculation and self-analysis, can hardly receive much
encouragement there; among the worst of intellectual sins is "re-
visionism." The very conditions under which the intellectual works
have made for a certain sterility.

In the ante-bellum South, the community's power was vested not
simply in a few men, but in white men everywhere—a pure instance of Mill's and Tocqueville's "tyranny of the majority." That

community, united on the essentials in stern democratic consensus, commanded a net of coercions that included everything from neighborly hostility to lynch law. A man might travel through the entire South, the Reverend Thornton Stringfellow noted approvingly in 1856, "and not find a single ism with an organized existence." The one crack (if such it may be called) in the wall of orthodoxy was an interesting difference of views over the new theory of plural origins of races, as opposed to the unity of creation theory set forth in Genesis. In a recent book about Josiah Nott and other plural-origins theorists of the period, much is made of Nott's intrepidity in braving the pulpit's displeasure on behalf of "science," as science was then understood. Yet one finds it difficult to take Nott's perils very seriously; his ideas were spread all over the South by DeBow and other publicists, and were snatched up with the liveliest interest. The Book of Genesis may have been one of the orthodoxies of the day, but the transcendent orthodoxy was slavery, and quibbles over how the races got started was a harmless bit of luxury so long as, on the main point, no compass needle deviated from due South. The peculiar fitness for slavery of the *Negro* race, whatever its origin, was denied by none. Had something truly fundamental been at issue, then Southern society, as perfectly organized to stifle heresy as has ever been the case anywhere, could be just as hard on its intellectuals, should they deviate from the path, as is Soviet society today.

And the intellectuals could be hard on each other, if any of their number did not come up to the work with every nerve stretched. Normally gentle persons such as George Frederick Holmes could turn themselves for the occasion into ruthless policemen. Holmes told his fellow Southerners in 1852 that they had bungled their handling of *Uncle Tom's Cabin,* whereupon he himself showed them how to deal with a peace-breaker like Harriet Beecher Stowe.* The critique of Northern capitalism, to be sure, took various interesting forms, as the modern reader will discover. Yet this aspect of proslavery thought, which to the twentieth century mind has been the most intriguing, was precisely the aspect that was buried first and

* For Holmes's review of *Uncle Tom's Cabin,* see below, pp. 99.

forgotten most readily by the South itself, once the Civil War and emancipation had rendered the main issue, slavery, meaningless.

One of the reasons was, of course, that the South was actually as capitalist-minded as the North. But the other was that the quality most prized so long as the argument went on was not, after all, creativity, but zeal. George Fitzhugh, who was nothing if not honest, gave the game away in 1857 when he wrote in *DeBow's* that although he differed "from what are called the extremists of the South," he "would not shoot down the sentinels of our camp." It was not really in their capacity as intellectuals that Fitzhugh— the South's leading intellectual—valued these men. "If not the wisest, most far-seeing, and most prudent," he admitted, "they are the most zealous friends of the South." Applying military metaphors to the realm of thought may be justified in special cases; conceivably this was one of them. But it seems clear, in any case, that safeguards for the right to speculate broadly and freely was not what Fitzhugh had in mind when he spoke of "sentinels."

JOHN C. CALHOUN (1782-1850)

DISQUISITION ON GOVERNMENT.

SPEECH ON THE RECEPTION OF ABOLITION PETITIONS.

SPEECH ON THE IMPORTANCE OF DOMESTIC SLAVERY.

ALTHOUGH THE SOUTH CAROLINA statesman did not write as extensively or systematically on slavery as did some of those who came after him, he was one
of the earliest exponents of the "positive good" attitude which dominated
the pro-slavery argument from the mid-1840s on. Much venerated by his
intellectual successors, John C. Calhoun left in his own written record most
of the ideas and attitudes in defense of slavery developed and elaborated by
others. The main ones may be found in the three excerpts given below. The
"Disquisition on Government," probably written in the early 1840s, was not
formally published until 1854, after his death. In it, Calhoun discusses the
proper balance between individual liberty and community power, saying that
the proportion must alter from community to community and that, for
peoples unfit to exercise it, too much liberty is a curse.

His "Speech on the Reception of Abolition Petitions," given in the Senate
on February 6, 1837, pronounces slavery "a good—a positive good." Echoing
Aristotle, he declares that no advanced community ever existed in which one
part did not live off the labor of the other. The conflict between labor and
capital is chronic, but the South with its slave system keeps the relationship
stable and quiet.

The third excerpt is from a speech made by Calhoun on January 10, 1838,
also in the Senate, in support of his own resolutions defining the constitutional relations of the states. Here he puts a special emphasis on the harmony
of capital and labor which characterizes the typical Southern plantation.

DISQUISITION ON GOVERNMENT.

. . . To PERFECT SOCIETY, it is necessary to develop the faculties, intellectual and moral, with which man is endowed. But the main spring to their development, and, through this, to progress, improvement and civilization, with all their blessings, is the desire of individuals to better their condition. For this purpose, liberty and security are indispensable. Liberty leaves each free to pursue the course he may deem best to promote his interest and happiness, as far as it may be compatible with the primary end for which government is ordained;—while security gives assurance to each, that he shall not be deprived of the fruits of his exertions to better his condition. These combined, give to this desire the strongest impulse of which it is susceptible. For, to extend liberty beyond the limits assigned, would be to weaken the government and to render it incompetent to fulfil its primary end,—the protection of society against dangers, internal and external. The effect of this would be, insecurity; and, of insecurity,—to weaken the impulse of individuals to better their condition, and thereby retard progress and improvement. On the other hand, to extend the powers of the government, so as to contract the sphere assigned to liberty, would have the same effect, by disabling individuals in their efforts to better their condition.

Herein is to be found the principle which assigns to power and liberty their proper spheres, and reconciles each to the other under all circumstances. For, if power be necessary to secure to liberty the fruits of its exertions, liberty, in turn, repays power with interest, by increased population, wealth, and other advantages, which progress and improvement bestow on the community. By thus assigning to each its appropriate sphere, all conflicts between

R. K. Crallé, ed., *The Works of John C. Calhoun,* I (New York: D. Appleton, 1854), 52-59. The entire "Disquisition," which includes Calhoun's famous "concurrent majority" theory, is 107 pages long.

them cease; and each is made to co-operate with and assist the other, in fulfilling the great ends for which government is ordained.

But the principle, applied to different communities, will assign to them different limits. It will assign a larger sphere to power and a more contracted one to liberty, or the reverse, according to circumstances. To the former, there must ever be allotted, under all circumstances, a sphere sufficiently large to protect the community against danger from without and violence and anarchy within. The residuum belongs to liberty. More cannot be safely or rightly allotted to it.

But some communities require a far greater amount of power than others to protect them against anarchy and external dangers; and, of course, the sphere of liberty in such, must be proportionally contracted. The causes calculated to enlarge the one and contract the other, are numerous and various. Some are physical;—such as open and exposed frontiers, surrounded by powerful and hostile neighbors. Others are moral;—such as the different degrees of intelligence, patriotism, and virtue among the mass of the community, and their experience and proficiency in the art of self-government. Of these, the moral are, by far, the most influential. A community may possess all the necessary moral qualifications, in so high a degree, as to be capable of self-government under the most adverse circumstances; while, on the other hand, another may be so sunk in ignorance and vice, as to be incapable of forming a conception of liberty, or of living, even when most favored by circumstances, under any other than an absolute and despotic government.

The principle, in all communities, according to these numerous and various causes, assigns to power and liberty their proper spheres. To allow to liberty, in any case, a sphere of action more extended than this assigns, would lead to anarchy; and this, probably, in the end, to a contraction instead of an enlargement of its sphere. Liberty, then, when forced on a people unfit for it, would, instead of a blessing, be a curse; as it would, in its reaction, lead directly to anarchy,—the greatest of all curses. No people, indeed, can long enjoy more liberty than that to which their situation and advanced intelligence and morals fairly entitle them. If more than this be allowed, they must soon fall into confusion and disorder,—to be followed, if not by anarchy and despotism, by a change to a form of government more simple and absolute; and, therefore, better suited to their condition. And hence, although it may be true, that a people may not have as much liberty as they are fairly entitled to, and are capable of enjoying,—yet the reverse is unquestionably true,—that no people can long possess more than they are fairly entitled to. .

Liberty, indeed, though among the greatest of blessings, is not so great as that of protection; inasmuch, as the end of the former is the progress and improvement of the race,—while that of the latter is its preservation and perpetuation. And hence, when the two come into conflict, liberty must, and ever ought, to yield to protection; as the existence of the race is of greater moment than its improvement.

It follows, from what has been stated, that it is a great and dangerous error to suppose that all people are equally entitled to liberty. It is a reward to be earned, not a blessing to be gratuitously lavished on all alike;—a reward reserved for the intelligent, the patriotic, the virtuous and deserving;—and not a boon to be bestowed on a people too ignorant, degraded and vicious, to be capable either of appreciating or of enjoying it. Nor is it any disparagement to liberty, that such is, and ought to be the case. On the contrary, its greatest praise,—its proudest distinction is, that an all-wise Providence has reserved it, as the noblest and highest reward for the development of our faculties, moral and intellectual. A reward more appropriate than liberty could not be conferred on the deserving;—nor a punishment inflicted on the undeserving more just, than to be subject to lawless and despotic rule. This dispensation seems to be the result of some fixed law;—and every effort to disturb or defeat it, by attempting to elevate a people in the scale of liberty, above the point to which they are entitled to rise, must ever prove abortive, and end in disappointment. The progress of a people rising from a lower to a higher point in the scale of liberty, is necessarily slow;—and by attempting to precipitate, we either retard, or permanently defeat it.

There is another error, not less great and dangerous, usually associated with the one which has just been considered. I refer to the opinion, that liberty and equality are so intimately united, that liberty cannot be perfect without perfect equality.

That they are united to a certain extent,—and that equality of citizens, in the eyes of the law, is essential to liberty in a popular government, is conceded. But to go further, and make equality of *condition* essential to liberty, would be to destroy both liberty and progress. The reason is, that inequality of condition, while it is a necessary consequence of liberty, is, at the same time, indispensable to progress. In order to understand why this is so, it is necessary to bear in mind, that the main spring to progress is, the desire of individuals to better their condition; and that the strongest impulse which can be given to it is, to leave individuals free to exert themselves in the manner they may deem best for that purpose, as far at least as it can be done consistently with the ends for which government is ordained,—and to secure to all the fruits of their exertions. Now, as individuals differ greatly from each other, in intelligence, sagacity, energy, perseverance, skill, habits of industry and economy, physical power, position and opportunity,—the necessary effect of leaving all free to exert themselves to better their condition, must be a corresponding inequality between those who may possess these qualities and advantages in a high degree, and those who may be deficient in them. The only means by which this result can be prevented are, either to impose such restrictions on the exertions of those who may possess them in a high degree, as will place them on a level with those who do not; or to deprive them of the fruits of their exertions. But to impose such restrictions on them would be destructive of liberty,—while, to deprive them of the fruits of their exertions, would be to destroy the desire of bettering their condition. It is, indeed, this inequality of condition between the front and rear ranks, in the march of progress, which gives so strong an impulse to the former to maintain their position, and to the latter to press forward into their files. This gives to progress its greatest impulse. To force the front rank back to the rear, or attempt to push forward the rear into line with the front, by the interposition of the government, would put an end to the impulse, and effectually arrest the march of progress.

These great and dangerous errors have their origin in the prevalent opinion that all men are born free and equal;—than which nothing can be more unfounded and false. It rests upon the assumption of a fact, which is contrary to universal observation, in whatever light it may be regarded. It is, indeed, difficult to explain how an opinion so destitute of all sound reason, ever could have been so extensively entertained, unless we regard it as being confounded with another, which has some semblance of truth;—but which, when properly understood, is not less false and dangerous. I refer to the assertion, that all men are equal in the state of nature; meaning, by a state of nature, a state of individuality, supposed to have existed prior to the social and political state; and in which men lived apart and independent of each other. If such a state ever did exist, all men would have been, indeed, free and equal in it; that is, free to do as they pleased, and exempt from the authority or control of others—as, by supposition, it existed anterior to society and government. But such a state is purely hypothetical. It never did, nor can exist; as it is inconsistent with the preservation and perpetuation of the race. It is, therefore, a great misnomer to call it *the state of nature*. Instead of being the natural state of man, it is, of all conceivable states, the most opposed to his nature—most repugnant to his feelings, and most incompatible with his wants. His natural state is, the social and political—the one for which his Creator made him, and the only one in which he can preserve and perfect his race. As, then, there never was such a state as the, so called, state of nature, and never can be, it follows, that men, instead of being born in it, are born in the social and political state; and of course, instead of being born free and equal, are born subject, not only to parental authority, but to the laws and institutions of the country where born and under whose protection they draw their first breath. . . .

SPEECH ON THE RECEPTION
OF ABOLITION PETITIONS.

. . . However sound the great body of the non-slaveholding States are at present, in the course of a few years they will be succeeded by those who will have been taught to hate the people and institutions of nearly one-half of this Union, with a hatred more deadly than one hostile nation ever entertained towards another. It is easy to see the end. By the necessary course of events, if left to themselves, we must become, finally, two people. It is impossible under the deadly hatred which must spring up between the two great sections, if the present causes are permitted to operate unchecked, that we should continue under the same political system. The conflicting elements would burst the Union asunder, powerful as are the links which hold it together. Abolition and the Union cannot co-exist. As the friend of the Union I openly proclaim it,—and the sooner it is known the better. The former may now be controlled, but in a short time it will be beyond the power of man to arrest the course of events. We of the South will not, cannot surrender our institutions. To maintain the existing relations between the two races, inhabiting that section of the Union, is indispensable to the peace and happiness of both. It cannot be subverted without drenching the country in blood, and extirpating one or the other of the races. Be it good or bad, it has grown up with our society and institutions, and is so interwoven with them, that to destroy it would be to destroy us as a people. But let me not be understood as admitting, even by implication, that the existing relations between the two races in the slaveholding States is an evil:—far otherwise; I hold it to be a good, as it has thus far proved itself to be to both, and will continue to prove so if

U. S. Senate, February 6, 1837. *Works*, II (New York: D. Appleton, 1856), 629-33, incompletely reported in *Congressional Globe*, 24 Cong., 2 Sess., p. 158.

not disturbed by the fell spirit of abolition. I appeal to facts. Never before has the black race of Central Africa, from the dawn of history to the present day, attained a condition so civilized and so improved, not only physically, but morally and intellectually. It came among us in a low, degraded, and savage condition, and in the course of a few generations it has grown up under the fostering care of our institutions, reviled as they have been, to its present comparatively civilized condition. This, with the rapid increase of numbers, is conclusive proof of the general happiness of the race, in spite of all the exaggerated tales to the contrary.

In the mean time, the white or European race has not degenerated. It has kept pace with its brethren in other sections of the Union where slavery does not exist. It is odious to make comparison; but I appeal to all sides whether the South is not equal in virtue, intelligence, patriotism, courage, disinterestedness, and all the high qualities which adorn our nature. I ask whether we have not contributed our full share of talents and political wisdom in forming and sustaining this political fabric; and whether we have not constantly inclined most strongly to the side of liberty, and been the first to see and first to resist the encroachments of power. In one thing only are we inferior—the arts of gain; we acknowledge that we are less wealthy than the Northern section of this Union, but I trace this mainly to the fiscal action of this Government, which has extracted much from, and spent little among us. Had it been the reverse,—if the exaction had been from the other section, and the expenditure with us, this point of superiority would not be against us now, as it was not at the formation of this Government.

But I take higher ground. I hold that in the present state of civilization, where two races of different origin, and distinguished by color, and other physical differences, as well as intellectual, are brought together, the relation now existing in the slaveholding States between the two, is, instead of an evil, a good—a positive good. I feel myself called upon to speak freely upon the subject where the honor and interests of those I represent are involved. I hold then, that there never has yet existed a wealthy and civilized society in which one portion of the community did not, in point of fact, live on the labor of the other. Broad and general as is this

assertion, it is fully borne out by history. This is not the proper
occasion, but if it were, it would not be difficult to trace the various
devices by which the wealth of all civilized communities has been
so unequally divided, and to show by what means so small a share
has been allotted to those by whose labor it was produced, and so
large a share given to the non-producing classes. The devices are
almost innumerable, from the brute force and gross superstition of
ancient times, to the subtle and artful fiscal contrivances of modern.
I might well challenge a comparison between them and the more
direct, simple, and patriarchal mode by which the labor of the
African race is, among us, commanded by the European. I may say
with truth, that in few countries so much is left to the share of
the laborer, and so little exacted from him, or where there is more
kind attention paid to him in sickness or infirmities of age. Compare his condition with the tenants of the poor houses in the more
civilized portions of Europe—look at the sick, and the old and
infirm slave, on one hand, in the midst of his family and friends,
under the kind superintending care of his master and mistress, and
compare it with the forlorn and wretched condition of the pauper
in the poor house. But I will not dwell on this aspect of the question;
I turn to the political; and here I fearlessly assert that the existing
relation between the two races in the South, against which these
blind fanatics are waging war, forms the most solid and durable
foundation on which to rear free and stable political institutions. It
is useless to disguise the fact. There is and always has been in an
advanced stage of wealth and civilization, a conflict between labor
and capital. The condition of society in the South exempts us from
the disorders and dangers resulting from this conflict; and which
explains why it is that the political condition of the slaveholding
States has been so much more stable and quiet than that of the
North. The advantages of the former, in this respect, will become
more and more manifest if left undisturbed by interference from
without, as the country advances in wealth and numbers. We have,
in fact, but just entered that condition of society where the strength
and durability of our political institutions are to be tested; and I
venture nothing in predicting that the experience of the next genera-

tion will fully test how vastly more favorable our condition of society is to that of other sections for free and stable institutions, provided we are not disturbed by the interference of others, or shall have sufficient intelligence and spirit to resist promptly and successfully such interference. It rests with ourselves to meet and repel them. I look not for aid to this Government, or to the other States; not but there are kind feelings towards us on the part of the great body of the non-slaveholding States; but as kind as their feelings may be, we may rest assured that no political party in these States will risk their ascendency for our safety. If we do not defend ourselves none will defend us; if we yield we will be more and more pressed as we recede; and if we submit we will be trampled under foot. Be assured that emancipation itself would nót satisfy these fanatics:—that gained, the next step would be to raise the negroes to a social and political equality with the whites; and that being effected, we would soon find the present condition of the two races reversed. They and their northern allies would be the masters, and we the slaves; the condition of the white race in the British West India Islands, bad as it is, would be happiness to ours. There the mother country is interested in sustaining the supremacy of the European race. It is true that the authority of the former master is destroyed, but the African will there still be a slave, not to individuals but to the community,—forced to labor, not by the authority of the overseer, but by the bayonet of the soldiery and the rod of the civil magistrate.

Surrounded as the slaveholding States are with such imminent perils, I rejoice to think that our means of defence are ample, if we shall prove to have the intelligence and spirit to see and apply them before it is too late. All we want is concert, to lay aside all party differences, and unite with zeal and energy in repelling approaching dangers. Let there be concert of action, and we shall find ample means of security without resorting to secession or disunion. I speak with full knowledge and a thorough examination of the subject, and for one, see my way clearly. One thing alarms me—the eager pursuit of gain which overspreads the land, and which absorbs every faculty of the mind and every feeling of the heart. Of all passions avarice is the most blind and compromising—the last to see and the first to yield to danger. I dare not hope that any thing I can say will arouse the South to a due sense of danger; I fear it is beyond the power of mortal voice to awaken it in time from the fatal security into which it has fallen.

SPEECH ON THE IMPORTANCE OF DOMESTIC SLAVERY.

CALHOUN'S RESOLUTIONS:

Resolved, That in the adoption of the Federal Constitution, the States adopting the same acted severally, as free, independent, and sovereign States; and that each, for itself, by its own voluntary assent, entered the Union with the view to its increased security against all dangers, *domestic* as well as foreign, and the more perfect and secure enjoyment of its advantages, natural, political, and social.

Resolved, That in delegating a portion of their powers to be exercised by the Federal Government, the States retained, severally, the exclusive and sole right over their own domestic institutions and police, and are alone responsible for them, and that any inter-meddling of any one or more States, or a combination of their citizens, with the domestic institutions and police of the others, on any ground, or under any pretext whatever, political, moral, or religious, with the view to their alteration, or subversion, is an assumption of superiority not warranted by the Constitution, in-sulting to the States interfered with, tending to endanger their domestic peace and tranquility, subversive of the objects for which the Constitution was formed, and, by necessary consequence, tend-ing to weaken and destroy the Union itself.

U. S. Senate, January 10, 1838. *Congressional Globe,* 25 Cong., 2 Sess., Appendix, pp. 61–62. The resolutions, introduced December 27, 1837, are in *ibid.,* p. 55. The speech given here is the one Calhoun made in support of the fourth resolution.

Resolved, That this Government was instituted and adopted by the several States of this Union as a common agent, in order to carry into effect the powers which they had delegated by the Constitution for their mutual security and prosperity; and that, in fulfilment of this high and sacred trust, this Government is bound so to exercise its powers as to give, as far as may be practicable, increased stability and security to the domestic institutions of the States that compose the Union; and that it is the solemn duty of the Government to resist all attempts by one portion of the Union to use it as an instrument to attack the domestic institutions of another, or to weaken or destroy such institutions, instead of strengthening and upholding them, as it is in duty bound to do.

Resolved, That domestic slavery, as it exists in the Southern and Western States of this Union, composes an important part of their domestic institutions, inherited from their ancestors, and existing at the adoption of the Constitution, by which it is recognised as constituting an essential element in the distribution of its powers among the States; and that no change of opinion, or feeling, on the part of the other States of the Union in relation to it, can justify them or their citizens in open and systematic attacks thereon, with the view to its overthrow; and that all such attacks are in manifest violation of the mutual and solemn pledge to protect and defend each other, given by the States, respectively, on entering into the Constitutional compact, which formed the Union, and as such is a manifest breach of faith, and a violation of the most solemn obligations, moral and religious.

Resolved, That the intermeddling of any State or States, or their citizens, to abolish slavery in this District, or any of the Territories, on the ground, or under the pretext, that it is immoral or sinful; or the passage of any act or measure of Congress, with that view, would be a direct and dangerous attack on the institutions of all the slaveholding States.

Resolved, That the union of these States rests on an equality of rights and advantages among its members; and that whatever destroys that equality, tends to destroy the Union itself; and that it is the solemn duty of all, and more especially of this body, which represents the States in their corporate capacity, to resist all attempts to discriminate between the States in extending the benefits of the Government to the several portions of the Union; and that to refuse to extend to the Southern and Western States any advantage which would tend to strengthen, or render them more secure, or increase their limits or population by the annexation of new territory or States, on the assumption or under the pretext that the institution of slavery, as it exists among them, is immoral or sinful, or otherwise obnoxious, would be contrary to that equality of rights and advantages which the Constitution was intended to secure alike to all the members of the Union, and would, in effect, disfranchise the slaveholding States, withholding from them the advantages, while it subjected them to the burthens, of the Government.

SPEECH OF JANUARY 10, 1838.

He saw (said Mr. C.) in the question before us the fate of the South. It was a higher than the mere naked question of master and slave. It involved a great political institution, essential to the peace and existence of one-half of this Union. A mysterious Providence had brought together two races, from different portions of the globe, and placed them together in nearly equal numbers in the Southern portion of this Union. They were there inseparably united, beyond the possibility of separation. Experience had shown that the existing relation between them secured the peace and happiness of both. Each had improved; the inferior greatly; so much so, that it had attained a degree of civilization never before attained by the black race in any age or country. Under no other relation could they co-exist together. To destroy it was to involve a whole region in slaughter, carnage, and desolation; and, come what will, we must defend and preserve it.

This agitation has produced one happy effect at least; it has compelled us to the South to look into the nature and character of this great institution, and to correct many false impressions that even we had entertained in relation to it. Many in the South once believed that it was a moral and political evil; that folly and delusion are gone; we see it now in its true light, and regard it as the most safe

and stable basis for free institutions in the world. It is impossible
with us that the conflict can take place between labor and capital,
which make it so difficult to establish and maintain free institutions in all wealthy and highly civilized nations where such institutions as ours do not exist. The Southern States are an aggregate, in
fact, of communities, not of individuals. Every plantation is a little
community, with the master at its head, who concentrates in himself the united interests of capital and labor, of which he is the
common representative. These small communities aggregated make
the State in all, whose action, labor, and capital is equally represented and perfectly harmonized. Hence the harmony, the union,
and stability of that section, which is rarely disturbed through the
action of this Government. The blessing of this state of things extends beyond the limits of the South. It makes that section the
balance of the system; the great conservative power, which prevents other portions, less fortunately constituted, from rushing into
conflict. In this tendency to conflict in the North between labor and
capital, which is constantly on the increase, the weight of the South
has and will ever be found on the Conservative side; against the
aggression of one or the other side, which ever may tend to disturb
the equilibrium of our political system. This is our natural position,
the salutary influence of which has thus far preserved, and will long
continue to preserve, our free institutions, if we should be left undisturbed. Such are the institutions which these deluded madmen
are stirring heaven and earth to destroy, and which we are called on
to defend by the highest and most solemn obligations that can be
imposed on us as men and patriots.

THOMAS R. DEW (1802-1846)

REVIEW OF THE DEBATE
IN THE VIRGINIA LEGISLATURE.

A TURNING POINT IN THE South's attitude toward slavery seems to have been
reached very early in the 1830s. Before that time, there was something
equivocal and defensive in pro-slavery sentiment; afterward, that sentiment
assumed a character ever more positive, assertive, and militant. One of the
precipitating elements was a series of debates in the Virginia legislature
during the winter of 1831-1832, in which the question of compensated emancipation of slaves and colonization of free Negroes was settled negatively
once and for all. Among the aftereffects of this debate was an unusually
able pamphlet by Thomas R. Dew, a professor of political economy and
other subjects at William and Mary College.

First published in 1832, Dew's Review of the Debate achieved immediate
influence, and during the next three decades it was often acknowledged by
Dew's intellectual successors as a model effort in the theoretical justification
of slavery.

Dew was not under quite the sort of pressure to which later Southern
writers were subjected, and this shows in the comparatively temperate tone
of his essay. He undertakes to justify slavery positively from a number of
angles, but one of the most interesting sections of the work—the one reprinted here—is simply an effort to show what might happen if slavery were
done away with. The argument, which explicitly appeals to Burke, is conservative rather than reactionary: the institutional disruptions of emancipation, Dew tries to explain, would outweigh any of its benefits.

. . . No SET OF LEGISLATORS ever have, or ever can, legislate upon
purely abstract principles, entirely independent of circumstances,
without the ruin of the body politic, which should have the mis-
fortune to be under the guidance of such quackery. Well and philo-

Review of the Debate in the Virginia Legislature of 1831 and 1832 (Richmond:
T. W. White, 1832), pp. 46-130, passim; reprinted in The Pro-Slavery Argument; as Maintained by . . . Chancellor Harper, Governor Hammond, Dr.
Simms, and Professor Dew (Charleston: Walker, Richards & Co., 1852), pp.
355-490, passim.

sophically has Burke remarked, that circumstances give in reality to every political principle its distinguishing color and discriminating effect. The circumstances are what render every political scheme beneficial or noxious to mankind, and we cannot stand forward and give praise or blame to anything which relates to human actions and human concerns, on a simple view of the object as it stands, stript of every relation, in all the nakedness and solitude of metaphysical abstraction. The historical view which we have given of the origin and progress of slavery, shows most conclusively that something else is requisite to convert slavery into freedom, than the mere enunciation of abstract truths, divested of all adventitious circumstances and relations. We shall now proceed to the second great division of our subject, and inquire seriously and fairly, whether there be any means by which we may get rid of slavery.

II. *Plans for the Abolition of Negro Slavery.*—Under this head we will examine first, those schemes which propose abolition and deportation; and secondly, those which contemplate emancipation without deportation.

1st. *Emancipation and Deportation.*—In the late Virginia Legislature, where the subject of slavery underwent the most thorough discussion, all seemed to be perfectly agreed in the necessity of removal in case of emancipation. Several members from the lower counties, which are deeply interested in this question, seemed to be sanguine in their anticipations of the final success of some project of emancipation and deportation to Africa, the original home of the negro. "Let us translate them," said one of the most respected and able members of the Legislature, (Gen. Broadnax,) "to those realms from which, in evil times, under inauspicious influences, their fathers were unfortunately abducted. . . ."

. . . Fortunately for reason and common sense, all these projects of deportation may be subjected to the most rigid and accurate calculations, which are amply sufficient to dispel all doubt, even in the minds of the most sanguine, as to their practicability.

We take it for granted, that the right of the owner to his slave is to be respected, and, consequently, that he is not required to emancipate him, unless his full value is paid by the State. Let us, then, keeping this in view, proceed to the very simple calculation of the

expense of emancipation and deportation in Virginia. The slaves, by
the last census (1830,) amounted within a small fraction to 470,000;
the average value of each one of these is, $200; consequently, the
whole aggregate value of the slave population of Virginia, in 1830,
was $94,000,000; and allowing for the increase since, we cannot err
far in putting the present value at $100,000,000. The assessed value
of all the houses and lands in the State, amounts to $206,000,000,
and these constitute the material items in the wealth of the State,
the whole personal property besides bearing but a very small proportion to the value of slaves, lands, and houses. Now, do not these
very simple statistics speak volumes upon this subject? It is gravely
recommended to the State of Virginia to give up a species of property which constitutes nearly one-third of the wealth of the whole
State, and almost one-half of that of Lower Virginia. and with the
remaining two-thirds to encounter the additional enormous expense
of transportation and colonization on the coast of Africa. But the
loss of $100,000,000 of property is scarcely the half of what Virginia
would lose, if the immutable laws of nature could suffer (as fortunately they cannot) this tremendous scheme of colonization to be
carried into full effect. . . .

. . . It is, in truth, the slave labor in Virginia which gives value
to her soil and her habitations; take away this, and you pull down
the Atlas that upholds the whole system; eject from the State the
whole slave population, and we risk nothing in the prediction, that
on the day in which it shall be accomplished, the worn soils of Virginia would not bear the paltry price of the government lands in the
West, and the Old Dominion will be a "waste howling wilderness";
—"the grass shall be seen growing in the streets, and the foxes
peeping from their holes."

But the favorers of this scheme say they do not contend for the
sudden emancipation and deportation of the whole black population;
they would send off only the increase, and thereby keep down the
population to its present amount, while the whites, increasing at
their usual rate, would finally become relatively so numerous as to
render the presence of the blacks among us for ever afterwards
entirely harmless. This scheme, which at first, to the unreflecting,
seems plausible, and much less wild than the project of sending off

the whole, is nevertheless impracticable and visionary, as we think a few remarks will prove. It is computed that the annual increase of the slaves and free colored population of Virginia is about six thousand. Let us first, then, make a calculation of the expense of purchase and transportation. At $200 each, the six thousand will amount in value to $1,200,000. At $30 each, for transportation, which we shall soon see is too little, we have the whole expense of purchase and transportation $1,380,000, an expense to be annually incurred by Virginia to keep down her black population to its present amount. And let us ask, is there any one who can seriously argue that Virginia can incur such an annual expense as this for the next twenty-five or fifty years, until the whites have multiplied so greatly upon the blacks, as, in the *opinion* of the *alarmists,* for ever to quiet the fears of the community? Vain and delusive hope, if any were ever wild enough to entertain it! Poor old Virginia! . . .

But this does not develop, to its full extent, the monstrous absurdity of this scheme. There is a view of it yet to be taken, which seems not to have struck very forcibly any of the speakers in the Virginia Legislature, but which appears to us, of itself perfectly conclusive against this whole project. . . . Virginia is, in fact, a *negro* raising State for other States; she produces enough for her own supply, and six thousand for sale. Now, suppose the government of Virginia enters the slave market resolved to purchase six thousand for emancipation and deportation, is it not evident that it must overbid the Southern seeker, and thus take the very slaves who would have gone to the South? The very first operation, then, of this scheme, provided slaves be treated as property, is to arrest the current which has been hitherto flowing to the South, and to accumulate the evil in the State. As sure as the moon in her transit over the meridian arrests the current which is gliding to the ocean, so sure will the action of the Virginia government, in an attempt to emancipate and send off six thousand slaves, stop those who are annually going out of the State; and when six thousand are sent off in one year, (which we never expect to see,) it will be found, on investigation, that they are those who would have been sent out of the State by the operation of our slave trade, and to the utter astonishment and confusion of our abolitionists, the black population will be found advancing with its usual rapidity—the only operation of the scheme being to substitute our government, *alias, ourselves,* as purchasers, instead of the planters of the South. . . .

. . . We have already shown that the first operation of the plan, if slave property were rigidly respected and never taken without full compensation, would be to put a stop to the efflux from the State through other channels; but this would not be the only effect. Government entering into the market with individuals, would elevate the price of slaves beyond their natural value, and consequently, the raising of them would become an object of primary importance throughout the whole State. We can readily imagine that the price of slaves might become so great that each master would do all in his power to encourage marriage among them—would allow the females almost entire exception from labor, that they might the better breed and nurse—and would so completely concentrate his efforts upon this object, as to neglect other schemes and less productive sources of wealth. Under these circumstances, the prolific African might, no doubt, be stimulated to press hard upon one of the limits above stated, doubling in numbers in fifteen years; and such is the tendency which our abolition schemes, if seriously engaged in, will most undoubtedly produce; they will be certain to stimulate the procreative powers of that very race which they are aiming to diminish; they will enlarge and invigorate the very monster which they are endeavoring to stifle, and realize the beautiful but melancholy fable of Sisyphus, by an eternal renovation of hope and disappointment. If it were possible for Virginia to purchase and send off annually for the next twenty-five or fifty years, twelve thousand slaves, we should have very little hesitation in affirming, that the number of slaves in Virginia would not be at all lessened by the operation, and at the conclusion of the period such habits would be generated among our blacks, that for a long time after the cessation of the drain, population might advance so rapidly as to produce among us all the calamities and miseries of an overcrowded people. . . .

The *poverty* stricken master would rejoice in the prolificness of his female slave, but pray Heaven in its kindness to strike with barrenness his own spouse, lest, in the plenitude of his misfortunes, brought on by the wild and quixotic philanthropy of his government, he might see around him a numerous offspring unprovided for, and destined to galling indigence.

It is almost useless to inquire whether this deportation of slaves to Africa would, as some seem most strangely to anticipate, invite the whites of other States into the Commonwealth. Who would be disposed to enter a State with worn out soil, and a black population mortgaged to the payment of millions *per annum*, for the purpose of emancipation and deportation, when in the West the most luxuriant soils, unincumbered with heavy exactions, could be purchased for the paltry sum of $1.25 per acre?

Where, then, is that multitude of whites to come from, which the glowing fancy of orators has sketched out as flowing into and filling up the *vacuum* created by the removal of slaves? . . .

Against most of the great difficulties attendant on the plan of emancipation above examined, it was impossible for the abolitionists entirely to close their eyes; and it is really curious to pause a moment and examine some of the reflections and schemes by which Virginia was to be reconciled to the plan. We have been told that it would not be necessary to purchase all the slaves sent away—that many would be surrendered by their owners without an equivalent. "There are a number of slaveholders," said one who has all the lofty feeling and devoted patriotism which have hitherto so proudly characterized Virginia, "at this very time, I do not speak from vain conjecture, but from what I know from the best information, and this number would continue to increase, who would voluntarily surrender their slaves, if the State would provide the means of colonizing them elsewhere. And there would be again another class, I have already heard of many, while they could not afford to sacrifice the entire value of their slaves, would cheerfully compromise with the State for half their value." In the first place, we would remark, that the gentleman's anticipation would certainly prove delusive—the surrender of a very few slaves would enhance the importance and value of the residue, and make the owner much more reluctant to part with them. Let any farmer in Lower Virginia ask himself how many he can spare from his plantation—and he will be surprised to see how few can be dispensed with. If that intelligent gentleman, from the storehouse of his knowledge, would but call up the history of the past, he would see that *mere philanthropy*, with all her splendid boastings, has never yet accomplished one great scheme. . . . But it is strange, indeed, that gentlemen have never reflected, that the pecuniary loss to the State will be precisely the same, whether the negroes be purchased or gratuitously surrendered. In the latter case, the burthen is only shifted from the whole State to that portion where the surrender is made—thus, if we own $10,000 worth of this property, and surrender the whole to government, it is evident that we lose the amount of $10,000; and if the whole of Lower Virginia could at once be induced to give up all of this property, and it could be sent away, the only effect of this generosity and self-devotion would be to inflict the *blow* of *desolation* more exclusively on this portion of the State—the aggregate loss would be the same, the burthen would only be shifted from the whole to a part. . . .

Again: some have attempted to evade the difficulties by seizing on the increase of the negroes after a certain time. Thus, Mr. Randolph's plan proposed that all born after the year 1840, should be raised by their masters to the age of eighteen for the female, and twenty-one for the male, and then hired out, until the neat sum arising therefrom amounted to enough to send them away. Scarcely any one in the Legislature—we believe not even the author himself —entirely approved of this plan. It is obnoxious to the objections we have just been stating against voluntary surrender. It proposes to saddle the slaveholder with the whole burthen; it infringes directly the rights of property; it converts the fee simple possession of this kind of property into an estate for years; and it only puts off the great sacrifice required of the State to 1840, when most of the evils will occur that have already been described. In the meantime, it destroys the value of slaves, and with it all landed possessions— checks the productions of the State, imposes (when 1840 arrives) upon the master the intolerable and grievous burthen of raising his young slaves to the ages of eighteen and twenty-one, and then liberating them to be hired out under the superintendence of government, (the most miserable of all managers,) until the proceeds arising therefrom shall be sufficient to send them away. If any man, at all conversant with political economy, should ever anticipate the day when this shall happen, we can only say that his faith is great indeed, enough to remove mountains, and that he has studied in a totally different school from ourselves. . . .

We hope we have now satisfactorily proved the impracticability of sending off the whole of our slave population, or even the annual increase; and we think we have been enabled to do this, by pointing out only one-half the difficulties which attend the scheme. We have so far confined our attention to the expense and difficulty of purchasing the slaves, and sending them across the ocean. We have now to look a little to the recipient or territory to which the blacks are to be sent; and if we know any thing of the history and nature of colonization, we shall be completely upheld in the assertion, that the difficulties on this score are just as great and insurmountable as those which we have shown to be attendant on the purchase and deportation. We shall be enabled to prove, if we may use the expression, *a double impracticability* attendant on all these schemes.

The Impossibility of Colonizing the Blacks.—The whole subject of colonization is much more difficult and intricate than is generally imagined, and the difficulties are often very different from what would, on slight reflection, be anticipated. . . .

The expense of deportation to Africa we have estimated at thirty dollars; but when there is taken into the calculation the further expense of collecting in Virginia, of feeding, protecting, &c., in Africa, the amount swells beyond all calculation. Mr. Tazewell, in his able report on the colonization of free people on the African coast, represents this expense as certainly amounting to $100; and, judging from actual experience, was disposed to think $200 would fall below the fair estimate. If the Virginia scheme shall ever be adopted, we have no doubt that both these estimates will fall below the real expense. The annual cost of removing six thousand, instead of being $1,380,000, will swell beyond $2,400,000,—an expense sufficient to destroy the entire value of the whole property of Virginia. . . .

But, say some, if Virginia cannot accomplish this work, let us call upon the General Government for aid—let Hercules be requested to put his shoulders to the wheels, and roll us through the formidable *guagmire* of our difficulties. Delusive prospect! Corrupting scheme!

We will throw all constitutional difficulties out of view, and ask if
the Federal Government can be requested to undertake the expense
for Virginia, without encountering it for the whole slaveholding
population? And then, whence can be drawn the funds to purchase
more than two million of slaves, worth at the lowest calculation
$400,000,000; or if the increase alone be sent off, can Congress
undertake annually to purchase at least sixty thousand slaves, at an
expense of $12,000,000, and deport and colonize them at an expense
of twelve or fifteen millions more? . . .

. . . Our Colonization Society has been more than fifteen years at
work; it has purchased, according to its funds, a district of country
as congenial to the constitution of the black as any in Africa; it has,
as we have seen, frequently over-supplied the colony with emigrants; and mark the result, for it is worthy of all observation, there
now are not more than 2,000 or 2,500 inhabitants in Liberia! And
these are alarmed lest the Southampton insurrection may cause
such an emigration as to inundate the colony. When, then, in the
lapse of time, can we ever expect to build up a colony which can
receive sixty or ninety thousand slaves per annum? . . .

Mr. Bacon admits, that one thousand emigrants now thrown on
Liberia, would ruin it. We believe that every reflecting sober member of the Colonization Society will acknowledge that five hundred
annually, are fully as many as the colony can now receive. We will
assume this number, though no doubt greatly beyond the truth; and
we will admit further, (what we could easily demonstrate to be
much too liberal a concession,) that the capacity of the colony for
the reception of emigrants may be made to enlarge in a geometrical
ratio, equal to that of the rate of increase of the blacks in the
United States. Now, with these very liberal concessions on our part,
let us examine into the effect of the colonization scheme. At the end
of the first year, we shall have for the amount of the 60,000, increasing at the rate of three and a half per cent., 61,800; and sub-
tracting 500, we shall begin the second year with the number of
61,300, which, increasing at the rate of three and a half per centum,
gives 63,139 for the amount at the end of the second year. Proceeding thus, we obtain, at the end of twenty-five years, for the amount

of the 60,000, 101,208. The number taken away, that is the sum of
$500 + 500 \times 1,003 + 500 \times 1,003$, &c., will be 18,197. It is thus seen,
that in spite of the efforts of the colonization scheme, the bare annual increase of our slaves will produce 41,208 more than can be sent
off; which number, of course, must be added to the capital of 60,000;
and long, *very long*, before the colony in Africa, upon our system of
calculation, even could receive the increase upon this accumulating
capital, its capacity as a recipient would be checked by the limita-
tion of territory, and the rapid filling up of the population, both by
emigration and natural increase. And thus, by a simple arithmetical
calculation, we may be convinced that the effort to check even the
geometrical rate of increase, by sending off the increment upon the
annual increase of our slaves, is greatly more than we can accomplish, and must inevitably terminate in disappointment—more than
realizing the fable of the frog and the ox; for in this case we should
have the frog *swelling*, not for the purpose of rivalling the ox in
size, but to *swallow him down, horns and all!*

Seeing, then, that the effort to send away the increase, on even
the present increase of our slaves, must be vain and fruitless, how
stupendously absurd must be the project, proposing to send off the
whole increase, so as to keep down the negro population at its present amount! There are some things which man, arrayed in all his
"brief authority," cannot accomplish, and this is one of them. . . .

Emancipation without Deportation.—We candidly confess, that
we look upon this last mentioned scheme as much more practicable,
and likely to be forced upon us, than the former. We consider it, at
the same time, so fraught with danger and mischief both to the
whites and blacks—so utterly subversive of the welfare of the slaveholding country, in both an economical and moral point of view, that
we cannot, upon any principle of right or expediency, give it our
sanction. . . .

. . . Much was said in the Legislature of Virginia about superiority of free labor over slave, and perhaps, under certain circumstances, this might be true; but, in the present instance, the question is between *the relative amounts of labor which may be obtained
from slaves before and after their emancipation.* Let us, then, first

commence with our country, where, it is well known to everybody, that slave labor is vastly more efficient and productive than the labor of free blacks.

Taken as a whole class, the latter must be considered the most worthless and indolent of the citizens of the United States. It is well known that throughout the whole extent of our Union, they are looked upon as the very *drones* and *pests* of society. Nor does this character arise from the disabilities and disfranchisement by which the law attempts to guard against them. In the non-slaveholding States, where they have been more elevated by law, this kind of population is in a worse condition, and much more troublesome to society, than in the slaveholding, and especially in the planting States. Ohio, some years ago, formed a sort of land of promise for this deluded class, to which many have repaired from the slave-holding States,—and what has been the consequence? They have been most harshly expelled from that State, and forced to take refuge in a foreign land. Look through the Northern States, and mark the class upon whom the eye of the police is most steadily and constantly kept—see with what vigilance and care they are hunted down from place to place—and you cannot fail to see that idleness and improvidence are at the root of all their misfortunes. Not only does the experience of our own country illustrate this great fact, but others furnish abundant testimony. . . .

. . . In the free black, the principle of idleness and dissipation triumphs over that of accumulation and the desire to better our condition; the animal part of the man gains the victory over the moral, and he, consequently, prefers sinking down into the listless, inglorious repose of the brute creation, to rising to that energetic activity which can only be generated amid the multiplied, refined, and artificial wants of civilized society. The very conception which nine slaves in ten have of liberty, is that of idleness and sloth with the enjoyment of plenty; and we are not to wonder that they should hasten to practice upon their theory so soon as liberated. But the experiment has been sufficiently tried to prove most conclusively that the free black will work nowhere except by compulsion. . . .

The great evil, however, of these schemes of emancipation, remains yet to be told. They are admirably calculated to excite plots,

murders and insurrections; whether gradual or rapid in their operation, this is the inevitable tendency. In the former case, you disturb
the quiet and contentment of the slave who is left unemancipated;
and he becomes the midnight murderer to gain that fatal freedom
whose blessings he does not comprehend. In the latter case, want
and invidious distinction will prompt to revenge. Two totally different races, as we have before seen, cannot easily harmonize together,
and although we have no idea that any organized plan of insurrection or rebellion can ever secure for the black the superiority, even
when free, yet his idleness will produce want and worthlessness, and
his very worthlessness and degradation will stimulate him to deeds
of rapine and vengeance; he will oftener engage in plots and mas-
sacres, and thereby draw down on his devoted head, the vengeance
of the provoked whites. But one limited massacre is recorded in
Virginia history; let her liberate her slaves, and every year you
would hear of insurrections and plots, and every day would perhaps
record a murder; the melancholy tale of Southampton would not
alone blacken the page of our history, and make the tender mother
shed the tear of horror over her babe as she clasped it to her bosom;
others of a deeper dye would thicken upon us; those regions where
the brightness of polished life has dawned and brightened into full
day, would relapse into darkness, thick and full of horrors. . . .

III. Injustice and Evils of Slavery.—1st. It is said slavery is
wrong, in the *abstract* at least, and contrary to the spirit of Christianity. To this we answer as before, that any question must be
determined by its circumstances, and if, as really is the case, we
cannot get rid of slavery without producing a greater injury to both
the masters and slaves, there is no rule of conscience or revealed law
of God which *can* condemn us. The physician will not order the
spreading cancer to be extirpated, although it will eventually cause
the death of his patient, because he would thereby hasten the fatal
issue. So, if slavery had commenced even contrary to the laws of
God and man, and the sin of its introduction rested upon our heads,
and it was even carrying forward the nation by slow degrees to final
ruin—yet, if it were *certain* that an attempt to remove it would only
hasten and heighten the final catastrophe—that it was, in fact, a
"vulnus immedicabile" on the body politic which no legislation

could safely remove, then we would not only not be found to attempt the extirpation, but we would stand guilty of a high offence in the sight of both God and man, if we should rashly make the effort. But the original sin of introduction rests not on our heads, and we shall soon see that all those dreadful calamities which the false prophets of our day are pointing to, will never, in all probability, occur.

       .   .   .   .   .

But it is time to bring this long article to a close; it is upon a subject which we have most reluctantly discussed; but, as we have already said, the example was set from a higher quarter; the seal has been broken, and we therefore determined to enter fully into the discussion. If our positions be true, and it does seem to us they may be sustained by reasoning almost as conclusive as the demonstrations of the mathematician, it follows, that the time for emancipation has not yet arrived, and perhaps it never will. We hope, sincerely, that the intelligent sons of Virginia will ponder before they move—before they enter into a scheme which will destroy more than half Virginia's wealth, and drag her down from her proud and elevated station among the mean things of the earth,—and when, Samson-like, she shall, by this ruinous scheme, be shorn of all her power and all her glory, the passing stranger may at some future day exclaim,

> The Niobe of nations—there she stands,
> "Friendless and helpless in her voiceless woe."

Once more, then, do we call upon our statesmen to pause, ere they engage in this ruinous scheme. The power of man has limits, and he should never attempt impossibilities. We do believe it is beyond the power of man to separate the elements of our population, even if it were desirable. The deep and solid foundations of society cannot be broken up by the vain *fiat* of the legislator. We must recollect that the *laws* of Lycurgus were promulgated, the sublime eloquence of Demosthenes and Cicero was heard, and the glorious achievements of Epaminondas and Scipio were witnessed, in countries where slavery existed—without *for one moment* loosening the tie between master and slave. We must recollect, too, that Poland has been desolated; that Kosciusko, Sobieski, Scrynecki, have fought and bled for the cause of liberty in that country; that one of her monarchs annulled, *in words*, the tie between master and slave, and yet the *order of nature* has, in the end, vindicated itself, and the dependence between master and slave has scarcely for a moment ceased. We must recollect, in fine, that our own country has waded through two dangerous wars—that the thrilling eloquence of the Demosthenes of our land has been heard with rapture, exhorting to death, rather than slavery,—that the most liberal principles have ever been promulgated and sustained, in our deliberate bodies, and before our judicial tribunals—and the whole has passed by without breaking or tearing asunder the elements of our social fabric. Let us reflect on these things, and learn wisdom from experience; and know that the relations of society, generated by the *lapse of ages*, cannot be altered in a *day*.

GEORGE FITZHUGH (1806-1881)

SOCIOLOGY FOR THE SOUTH.

GEORGE FITZHUGH, the most noted of the pro-slavery intellectuals, spent virtually all his adult life in the modest rural isolation of Port Royal, Virginia. He practiced law intermittently and was the master of a rather shabby plantation there. From these pursuits he eked out no more than a competence, though his existence seems to have been a fairly contented one. He also held a Federal appointment during the Buchanan administration as law clerk in the Attorney-General's office, and after the war he served for a time as an associate judge of the Freedmen's Court in Virginia.

Yet Fitzhugh was primarily a writer and social philosopher. From about 1850 on, a good portion of his income was earned through his books and articles—the invariable subject of which was the virtues of a patriarchal way of life based on slavery. His is the classic Southern indictment of liberal capitalism. In his pages one may see, in its most fully developed form, the case for an organic set of "feudal" values transplanted to the nineteenth century, as well as the peculiar affinity between those values and the emergent doctrines of revolutionary socialism. Both the causes and consequences of that class warfare which free competition renders inevitable, according to Fitzhugh, can be alleviated only by a system of slavery.

The selection which follows was first published by Fitzhugh as a pamphlet in 1850; four years later it reappeared as part of his *Sociology for the South*.

LIBERTY AND EQUALITY are new things under the sun. The free states of antiquity abounded with slaves. The feudal system that supplanted Roman institutions changed the form of slavery, but brought with it neither liberty nor equality. France and the Northern States of our Union have alone fully and fairly tried the experiment of a social organization founded upon universal liberty and equality of rights. England has only approximated to this condition in her commercial and manufacturing cities. The examples of small communities in Europe are not fit exponents of the working of the

Slavery Justified, by a Southerner (Fredericksburg: Recorder Printing Office, 1850), later included in *Sociology for the South, or the Failure of Free Society* (Richmond: A. Morris, 1854), pp. 226-58 *passim*.

system. In France and in our Northern States the experiment has already failed, if we are to form our opinions from the discontent of the masses, or to believe the evidence of the Socialists, Communists, Anti-Renters, and a thousand other agrarian sects that have arisen in these countries, and threaten to subvert the whole social fabric. The leaders of these sects, at least in France, comprise within their ranks the greater number of the most cultivated and profound minds in the nation, who have made government their study. Add to the evidence of these social philosophers, who, watching closely the working of the system, have proclaimed to the world its total failure, the condition of the working classes, and we have conclusive proof that liberty and equality have not conduced to enhance the comfort or the happiness of the people. Crime and pauperism have increased. Riots, trade unions, strikes for higher wages, discontent breaking out into revolution, are things of daily occurrence, and show that the poor see and feel quite as clearly as the philosophers, that their condition is far worse under the new than under the old order of things. Radicalism and Chartism in England owe their birth to the free and equal institutions of her commercial and manufacturing districts, and are little heard of in the quiet farming districts, where remnants of feudalism still exist in the relation of landlord and tenant, and in the laws of entail and primogeniture.

So much for experiment. We will now endeavor to treat the subject theoretically, and to show that the system is on its face self-destructive and impracticable. When we look to the vegetable, animal and human kingdoms, we discover in them all a constant conflict, war, or race of competition, the result of which is, that the weaker or less healthy genera, species and individuals are continually displaced and exterminated by the stronger and more hardy. It is a means by which some contend Nature is perfecting her own work. We, however, witness the war, but do not see the improvement. Although from the earliest date of recorded history, one race of plants has been eating out and taking the place of another, the stronger or more cunning animals have been destroying the feebler, and man exterminating and supplanting his fellow, still the plants, the animals and the men of to-day seem not at all superior, even in those qualities of strength and hardihood to which they owe their continued existence, to those of thousands of years ago. To this propensity of the strong to oppress and destroy the weak, government owes its existence. So strong is this propensity, and so destructive to human existence, that man has never yet been found so savage as to be without government. Forgetful of this important fact, which is the origin of all governments, the political economists and the advocates of liberty and equality propose to enhance the well being of man by trammeling his conduct as little as possible, and encouraging what they call FREE COMPETITION. Now, free competition is but another name for liberty and equality, and we must acquire precise and accurate notions about it in order to ascertain how free institutions will work. It is, then, that war or conflict to which Nature impels her creatures, and which government was intended to restrict. It is true, it is that war somewhat modified and restricted, for the warmest friends of freedom would have some government. The question is, whether the proposed restrictions are sufficient to neutralize the self-destructive tendencies which nature impresses on society. We proceed to show that the war of the wits, of mind with mind, which free competition or liberty and equality beget and encourage, is quite as oppressive, cruel and exterminating, as the war of the sword, of theft, robbery, and murder, which it forbids. It is only substituting strength of mind for strength of body. Men are told it is their duty to compete, to endeavor to get ahead of and supplant their fellow men, by the exercise of all the intellectual and moral strength with which nature and education have endowed them. "Might makes right," is the order of creation, and this law of nature, so far as mental might is concerned, is restored by liberty to man. The struggle to better one's condition, to pull others down or supplant them, is the great organic law of free society. All men being equal, all aspire to the highest honors and the largest possessions. Good men and bad men teach their children one and the same lesson—"Go ahead, push your way in the world." In such society, virtue, if virtue there be, loses all her loveliness because of her selfish aims. None but the selfish virtues are encouraged, because none other aid a man in the race of free competition. Good men and bad men have the same end in view, are in pursuit of the same object—self-promotion, self-elevation. The good man is prudent, cautious, and cunning of fence; he knows well the arts (the virtues, if you please,) which will advance his fortunes and enable him to depress and supplant others; he bides his time, takes advantage of the follies, the improvidence, and vices of others, and makes his fortune out of the misfortunes of his fellow men. The bad man is rash, hasty, and unskillful. He is equally selfish, but not half so cunning. Selfishness is almost the only motive of human conduct with good and bad in free society, where every man is taught that he may change and better his condition. A vulgar adage, "Every man for himself, and devil take the hindmost," is the moral which liberty and free competition inculcate. Now, there are no more honors and wealth in proportion to numbers, in this generation, than in the one which preceded it; population fully keeps pace with the means of subsistence; hence, those who better their condition or rise to higher places in society, do so generally by pulling down others or pushing them from their places. Where men of strong minds, of strong wills, and of great self-control, come into free competition with the weak and improvident, the latter soon become the inmates of jails and penitentiaries.

The statistics of France, England and America show that pauperism and crime advance *pari passu* with liberty and equality. How can it be otherwise, when all society is combined to oppress the poor and weak minded? The rich man, however good he may be, employs the laborer who will work for the least wages. If he be a good man, his punctuality enables him to cheapen the wages of the poor man. The poor war with one another in the race of competition, in order to get employment, by underbidding; for laborers are more abundant than employers. Population increases faster than capital. . . .

We do not set children and women free because they are not capable of taking care of themselves, not equal to the constant struggle of society. To set them free would be to give the lamb to the wolf to take care of. Society would quickly devour them. If the children of ten years of age were remitted to all the rights of person and property which men enjoy, all can perceive how soon

ruin and penury would overtake them. But half of mankind are
but grown-up children, and liberty is as fatal to them as it would
be to children. . . .

One step more, and that the most difficult in this process of
reasoning and illustration, and we have done with this part of our
subject. Liberty and equality throw the whole weight of society on
its weakest members; they combine all men in oppressing precisely
that part of mankind who most need sympathy, aid and protection.
The very astute and avaricious man, when left free to exercise
his faculties, is injured by no one in the field of competition, but
levies a tax on all with whom he deals. The sensible and prudent,
but less astute man, is seldom worsted in competing with his fellow men, and generally benefited. The very simple and improvident
man is the prey of every body. The simple man represents a class,
the common day laborers. The employer cheapens their wages, and
the retail dealer takes advantage of their ignorance, their inability
to visit other markets, and their want of credit, to charge them
enormous profits. They bear the whole weight of society on their
shoulders; they are the producers and artificers of all the necessaries, the comforts, the luxuries, the pomp and splendor of the
world; they create it all, and enjoy none of it; they are the muzzled
ox that treadeth out the straw; they are at constant war with
those above them, asking higher wages but getting lower; for they
are also at war with each other, underbidding to get employment.
This process of underbidding never ceases so long as employers want
profits or laborers want employment. It ends when wages are reduced too low to afford subsistence, in filling poor-houses, and jails,
and graves. It has reached that point already in France, England
and Ireland. A half million died of hunger in one year in Ireland—
they died because in the eye of the law they were the equals, and
liberty had made them the enemies, of their landlords and employers. Had they been vassals or serfs, they would have been beloved,
cherished and taken care of by those same landlords and employers.
Slaves never die of hunger, scarcely ever feel want.

The bestowing upon men equality of rights, is but giving license
to the strong to oppress the weak. It begets the grossest inequalities
of condition. Menials and day laborers are and must be as numer-

ous as in a land of slavery. And these menials and laborers are
only taken care of while young, strong and healthy. If the laborer
gets sick, his wages cease just as his demands are greatest. If two
of the poor get married, who being young and healthy, are getting
good wages, in a few years they may have four children. Their
wants have increased, but the mother has enough to do to nurse the
four children, and the wages of the husband must support six. There
is no equality, except in theory, in such society, and there is no
liberty. The men of property, those who own lands and money,
are masters of the poor; masters, with none of the feelings, interests
or sympathies of masters; they employ them when they please,
and for what they please, and may leave them to die in the high-
way, for it is the only home to which the poor in free countries
are entitled. They (the property holders) beheaded Charles Stuart
and Louis Capet, because these kings asserted a divine right to
govern wrong, and forgot that office was a trust to be exercised for
the benefit of the governed; and yet they seem to think that property is of divine right, and that they may abuse its possession to
the detriment of the rest of society, as much as they please. A
pretty exchange the world would make, to get rid of kings who often
love and protect the poor, and get in their place a million of pelt-
ing, petty officers in the garb of money-changers and land-owners,
who think that as they own all the property, the rest of mankind
have no right to a living, except on the conditions they may pre-
scribe. " 'Tis better to fall before the lion than the wolf," and
modern liberty has substituted a thousand wolves for a few lions.
The vulgar landlords, capitalists and employers of to-day, have the
liberties and lives of the people more completely in their hands,
than had the kings, barons and gentlemen of former times; and
they hate and oppress the people as cordially as the people despise
them. But these vulgar parvenus, these psalm-singing regicides,
these worshipers of Mammon, "have but taught bloody instructions,
which being taught, return to plague the inventor." The king's office was a trust, so are your lands, houses and money. Society permits you to hold them, because private property well administered
conduces to the good of all society. *This is your only title;* you lose
your right to your property, as the king did to his crown, so soon

as you cease faithfully to execute your trust; you can't make commons and forests of your lands and starve mankind; you must manage your lands to produce the most food and raiment for mankind, or you forfeit your title; you may not understand this philosophy, but you feel that it is true, and are trembling in your seats as you hear the murmurings and threats of the starving poor.

The moral effect of free society is to banish Christian virtue, that virtue which bids us love our neighbor as ourself, and to substitute the very equivocal virtues proceeding from mere selfishness. The intense struggle to better each one's pecuniary condition, the rivalries, the jealousies, the hostilities which it begets, leave neither time nor inclination to cultivate the heart or the head. Every finer feeling of our nature is chilled and benumbed by its selfish atmosphere; affection is under the ban, because affection makes us less regardful of mere self; hospitality is considered criminal waste, chivalry a stumbling-block, and the code of honor foolishness; taste, sentiment, imagination, are forbidden ground, because no money is to be made by them. Gorgeous pageantry and sensual luxury are the only pleasures indulged in, because they alone are understood and appreciated, and they are appreciated just for what they cost in dollars and cents. What makes money, and what costs money, are alone desired. Temperance, frugality, thrift, attention to business, industry, and skill in making bargains are virtues in high repute, because they enable us to supplant others and increase our own wealth. The character of our Northern brethren, and of the Dutch, is proof enough of the justice of these reflections. The Puritan fathers had lived in Holland, and probably imported Norway rats and Dutch morality in the Mayflower.

Liberty and equality are not only destructive to the morals, but to the happiness of society. Foreigners have all remarked on the care-worn, thoughtful, unhappy countenances of our people, and the remark only applies to the North, for travellers see little of us at the South, who live far from highways and cities, in contentment on our farms.

The facility with which men may improve their condition would, indeed, be a consideration much in favor of free society, if it did not involve as a necessary consequence the equal facility and

liability to lose grade and fortune. As many fall as rise. The wealth
of society hardly keeps pace with its numbers. All cannot be
rich. The rich and the poor change places oftener than where there
are fixed hereditary distinctions; so often, that the sense of insecurity makes every one unhappy. . . .

. . . Those who rise, pull down a class as numerous, and often
more worthy than themselves, to the abyss of misery and penury.
Painful as it may be, the reader shall look with us at this dark
side of the picture, he shall view the vanquished as well as the
victors on this battle-ground of competition; he shall see those who
were delicately reared, taught no tricks of trade, no shifts of thrifty
avarice, spurned, insulted, down-trodden by the coarse and vulgar
whose wits and whose appetites had been sharpened by necessity.
If he can sympathize with fallen virtue or detest successful vice,
he will see nothing in this picture to admire.

In Boston, a city famed for its wealth and the prudence of its
inhabitants, nine-tenths of the men in business fail. In the slaveholding South, except in new settlements, failures are extremely
rare; small properties descend from generation to generation in the
same family; there is as much stability and permanency of property as is compatible with energy and activity in society; fortunes
are made rather by virtuous industry than by tricks, cunning and
speculation.

We have thus attempted to prove from theory and from actual
experiment, that a society of universal liberty and equality is absurd
and impracticable. We have performed our task, we know, indif-
ferently, but hope we have furnished suggestions that may be
profitably used by those more accustomed to authorship.

We now come in the order of our subject to treat of the various
new sects of philosophers that have appeared of late years in France
and in our free States, who, disgusted with society as it exists,
propose to re-organize it on entirely new principles. We have never
heard of a convert to any of these theories in the slave States. If
we are not all contented, still none see evils of such magnitude
in society as to require its entire subversion and reconstruction.
We shall group all these sects together, because they all concur in
the great truth that Free Competition is the bane of free society;

they all concur, too, in modifying or wholly destroying the institution of private property. Many of them, seeing that property enables its owners to exercise a more grinding oppression than kings ever did, would destroy its tenure altogether. In France, especially, these sects are headed by men of great ability, who saw the experiment of liberty and equality fairly tested in France after the revolution of 1792. They saw, as all the world did, that it failed to promote human happiness or well-being.

France found the Consulate and the Empire havens of bliss compared with the stormy ocean of liberty and equality on which she had been tossed. Wise, however, as these Socialists and Communists of France are, they cannot create a man, a tree, or a new system of society; these are God's works, which man may train, trim and modify, but cannot create. The attempt to establish government on purely theoretical abstract speculation, regardless of circumstance and experience, has always failed; never more signally than with the Socialists.

The frequent experience of the Abbé Sieyès' paper structures of government, which lasted so short a time, should have taught them caution; but they were bolder reformers than he; they had a fair field for their experiment after the expulsion of Louis Phillippe; they tried it, and their failure was complete and ridiculous. The Abbé's structures were adamant compared to theirs. The rule of the weak Louis Napoleon was welcomed as a fortunate escape from their schemes of universal benevolence, which issued in universal bankruptcy.

The sufferings of the Irish, and the complaints of the Radicals and Chartists, have given birth to a new party in England, called Young England. This party saw in the estrangement and hostility of classes, and the sufferings of the poor, the same evils of free competition that had given rise to Socialism in France; though less talented than the Socialists, they came much nearer discovering the remedy for these evils.

Young England belongs to the most conservative wing of the tory party; he inculcates strict subordination of rank; would have the employer kind, attentive and paternal, in his treatment of the operative. The operative, humble, affectionate and obedient to his employer. He is young, and sentimental, and would spread his doctrines in tracts, sonnets and novels; but society must be ruled by sterner stuff than sentiment. Self-interest makes the employer and free laborer enemies. The one prefers to pay low wages, the other needs high wages. War, constant war, is the result, in which the operative perishes, but is not vanquished; he is hydra-headed, and when he dies two take his place. But numbers diminish his strength. The competition among laborers to get employment begets an intestine war, more destructive than the war from above. There is but one remedy for this evil, so inherent in free society, and that is, to identify the interests of the weak and the strong, the poor and the rich. Domestic Slavery does this far better than any other institution. Feudalism only answered the purpose in so far as Feudalism retained the features of slavery. To it (slavery) Greece and Rome, Egypt and Judea, and all the other distinguished States of antiquity, were indebted for their great prosperity and high civilization. . . .

But this high civilization and domestic slavery did not merely co-exist, they were cause and effect. Every scholar whose mind is at all imbued with ancient history and literature, sees that Greece and Rome were indebted to this institution alone for the taste, the leisure and the means to cultivate their heads and their hearts; had they been tied down to Yankee notions of thrift, they might have produced a Franklin, with his "penny saved is a penny gained"; they might have had utilitarian philosophers and invented the spinning jenny, but they never would have produced a poet, an orator, a sculptor or an architect; they would never have uttered a lofty sentiment, achieved a glorious feat in war, or created a single work of art. . . .

And now Equality where are thy monuments? And Echo answers where! Echo deep, deep, from the bowels of the earth, where women and children drag out their lives in darkness, harnessed like horses to heavy cars loaded with ore. Or, perhaps, it is an echo from some grand, gloomy and monotonous factory, where pallid children work fourteen hours a day, and go home at night to sleep in damp cellars. It may be too, this cellar contains aged parents too old to work, and cast off by their employer to die. Great railroads and mighty steamships too, thou mayest boast, but still the operatives who construct them are beings destined to poverty and neglect. Not a vestige of art canst thou boast; not a ray of genius illumes thy handiwork. The sordid spirit of Mammon presides o'er all, and from all proceed the sighs and groans of the oppressed.

Domestic slavery in the Southern States has produced the same results in elevating the character of the master that it did in Greece and Rome. He is lofty and independent in his sentiments, generous, affectionate, brave and eloquent; he is superior to the Northerner in every thing but the arts of thrift. History proves this. . . . Scipio and Aristides, Calhoun and Washington, are the noble results of domestic slavery. Like Egyptian obelisks 'mid the waste of time—simple, severe, sublime,—they point ever heavenward, and lift the soul by their examples. . . .

But the chief and far most important enquiry is, how does slavery affect the condition of the slave? One of the wildest sects of Communists in France proposes not only to hold all property in common, but to divide the profits, not according to each man's input and labor, but according to each man's wants. Now this is precisely the system of domestic slavery with us. We provide for each slave, in old age and in infancy, in sickness and in health, not according to his labor, but according to his wants. The master's wants are more costly and refined, and he therefore gets a larger share of the profits. A Southern farm is the beau ideal of Communism; it is a joint concern, in which the slave consumes more than the master, of the coarse products, and is far happier, because although the concern may fail, he is always sure of a support; he is only transferred to another master to participate in the profits of another concern; he marries when he pleases, because he knows he will have to work no more with a family than without one, and whether he live or die, that family will be taken care of; he exhibits all the pride of ownership, despises a partner in a smaller concern, "a poor man's negro," boasts of "our crops, horses, fields and cattle;" and is as happy as a human being can be. And why should he not?—he enjoys as much of the fruits of the farm as he is capable of doing, and the wealthiest can do no more. Great wealth brings many additional cares, but few additional enjoy-

ments. Our stomachs do not increase in capacity with our fortunes.
We want no more clothing to keep us warm. We may create new
wants, but we cannot create new pleasures. The intellectual enjoy-
ments which wealth affords are probably balanced by the new
cares it brings along with it.

There is no rivalry, no competition to get employment among
slaves, as among free laborers. Nor is there a war between master
and slave. The master's interest prevents his reducing the slave's
allowance or wages in infancy or sickness, for he might lose the
slave by so doing. His feeling for his slave never permits him to
stint him in old age. The slaves are all well fed, well clad, have
plenty of fuel, and are happy. They have no dread of the future—
no fear of want. A state of dependence is the only condition in
which reciprocal affection can exist among human beings—the
only situation in which the war of competition ceases, and peace,
amity and good will arise. A state of independence always begets
more or less of jealous rivalry and hostility. A man loves his children because they are weak, helpless and dependent. He loves his
wife for similar reasons. When his children grow up and assert
their independence, he is apt to transfer his affection to his grand-
children. He ceases to love his wife when she becomes masculine
or rebellious; but slaves are always dependent, never the rivals of
their master. Hence, though men are often found at variance with
wife or children, we never saw one who did not like his slaves,
and rarely a slave who was not devoted to his master. "I am thy
servant!" disarms me of the power of master. Every man feels the
beauty, force and truth of this sentiment of Sterne. But he who
acknowledges its truth, tacitly admits that dependence is a tie of
affection, that the relation of master and slave is one of mutual
good will. Volumes written on the subject would not prove as much
as this single sentiment. It has found its way to the heart of every
reader, and carried conviction along with it. The slaveholder is
like other men; he will not tread on the worm nor break the
bruised reed. The ready submission of the slave, nine times out
of ten, disarms his wrath even when the slave has offended. The
habit of command may make him imperious and fit him for rule;
but he is only imperious when thwarted or crossed by his equals;

he would scorn to put on airs of command among blacks, whether slaves or free; he always speaks to them in a kind and subdued tone. We go farther, and say the slaveholder is better than others —because he has greater occasion for the exercise of the affections. His whole life is spent in providing for the minutest wants of others, in taking care of them in sickness and in health. Hence he is the least selfish of men. Is not the old bachelor who retires to seclusion, always selfish? Is not the head of a large family almost always kind and benevolent? And is not the slaveholder the head of the largest family? Nature compels master and slave to be friends; nature makes employers and free laborers enemies.

The institution of slavery gives full development and full play to the affections. Free society chills, stints and eradicates them. In a homely way the farm will support all, and we are not in a hurry to send our children into the world, to push their way and make their fortunes, with a capital of knavish maxims. We are better husbands, better fathers, better friends, and better neighbors than our Northern brethren. The tie of kindred to the fifth degree is often a tie of affection with us. First cousins are scarcely acknowledged at the North, and even children are prematurely pushed off into the world. Love for others is the organic law of our society, as self-love is of theirs.

Every social structure must have its substratum. In free society this substratum, the weak, poor and ignorant, is borne down upon and oppressed with continually increasing weight by all above. We have solved the problem of relieving this substratum from the pressure from above. The slaves are the substratum, and the master's feelings and interests alike prevent him from bearing down upon and oppressing them. With us the pressure on society is like that of air or water, so equally diffused as not any where to be felt. With them it is the pressure of the enormous screw, never yielding, continually increasing. Free laborers are little better than trespassers on this earth given by God to all mankind. The birds of the air have nests, and the foxes have holes, but they have not where to lay their heads. They are driven to cities to dwell in damp and crowded cellars, and thousands are even forced to lie in the open air. This accounts for the rapid growth of Northern cities.

The feudal Barons were more generous and hospitable and less tyrannical than the petty land-holders of modern times. Besides, each inhabitant of the barony was considered as having some right of residence, some claim to protection from the Lord of the Manor. A few of them escaped to the municipalities for purposes of trade, and to enjoy a larger liberty. Now penury and the want of a home drive thousands to towns. The slave always has a home, always an interest in the proceeds of the soil. . . .

In France, England, Scotland and Ireland, the genius of famine hovers o'er the land. Emigrants, like a flock of hungry pigeons or Egyptian locusts, are alighting on the North. Every green thing will soon be consumed. The hollow, bloated prosperity which she now enjoys is destined soon to pass away. Her wealth does not increase with her numbers; she is dependent for the very necessaries of life on the slaveholding States. If those States cut off commercial intercourse with her, as they certainly will do if she does not speedily cease interference with slavery, she will be without food or clothing for her overgrown population. She is already threatened with a social revolution. . . .

At the slaveholding South all is peace, quiet, plenty and contentment. We have no mobs, no trades unions, no strikes for higher wages, no armed resistance to the law, but little jealousy of the rich by the poor. We have but few in our jails, and fewer in our poor houses. We produce enough of the comforts and necessaries of life for a population three or four times as numerous as ours. We are wholly exempt from the torrent of pauperism, crime, agrarianism, and infidelity which Europe is pouring from her jails and alms houses on the already crowded North. Population increases slowly, wealth rapidly. . . . Wealth is more equally distributed than at the North, where a few millionaires own most of the property of the country. (These millionaires are men of cold hearts and weak minds; they know how to make money, but not how to use it, either for the benefit of themselves or of others.) High intellectual and moral attainments, refinement of head and heart, give standing to a man in the South, however poor he may be. Money is, with few exceptions, the only thing that ennobles at the North. We have poor among us, but none who are over-worked and under-fed. We do not crowd cities because lands are abundant and their owners kind, merciful and hospitable. The poor are as hospitable as the rich, the negro as the white man. Nobody dreams of turning a friend, a relative, or a stranger from his door. The very negro who deems it no crime to steal, would scorn to sell his hospitality. We have no loafers, because the poor relative or friend who borrows our horse, or spends a week under our roof, is a welcome guest. The loose economy, the wasteful mode of living at the South, is a blessing when rightly considered; it keeps want, scarcity and famine at a distance, because it leaves room for retrenchment. The nice, accurate economy of France, England and New England, keeps society always on the verge of famine, because it leaves no room to retrench, that is to live on a part only of what they now consume. Our society exhibits no appearance of precocity, no symptoms of decay. A long course of continuing improvement is in prospect before us, with no limits which human foresight can descry. Actual liberty and equality with our white population has been approached much nearer than in the free States. Few of our whites ever work as day laborers, none as cooks, scullions, ostlers, body servants, or in other menial capacities. One free citizen does not lord it over another; hence that feeling of independence and equality that distinguishes us; hence that pride of character, that self-respect, that gives us ascendancy when we come in contact with Northerners. It is a distinction to be a Southerner, as it was once to be a Roman citizen.

. . . Until the last fifteen years, our great error was to imitate Northern habits, customs and institutions. Our circumstances are so opposite to theirs, that whatever suits them is almost sure not to suit us. Until that time, in truth, we distrusted our social system. We thought slavery morally wrong, we thought it would not last, we thought it unprofitable. The Abolitionists assailed us; we looked more closely into our circumstances; became satisfied that slavery was morally right, that it would continue ever to exist, that it was as profitable as it was humane. This begat self-confidence, self-reliance. Since then our improvement has been rapid. Now we may safely say, that we are the happiest, most contented and prosperous people on earth. The intermeddling of foreign pseudo-philanthopists in our affairs, though it has occasioned great irritation and indignation, has been of inestimable advantage in teaching us to form a right estimate of our condition. This intermeddling will soon cease; the poor at home in thunder tones demand their whole attention and all their charity. Self-preservation will compel them to listen to their demands. Moreover, light is breaking in upon us from abroad. All parties in England now agree that the attempt to put down the slave trade has greatly aggravated its horrors, without at all diminishing the trade itself. It is proposed to withdraw her fleet from the African coast. France has already given notice that she will withdraw hers. America will follow the example. The emancipation of the slaves in the West Indies is admitted to have been a failure in all respects. The late masters have been ruined, the liberated slaves refuse to work, and are fast returning to the savage state, and England herself has sustained a severe blow in the present diminution and prospective annihilation of the once enormous imports from her West Indian colonies.

In conclusion, we will repeat the propositions, in somewhat different phraseology, with which we set out. First—That Liberty and Equality, with their concomitant Free Competition, beget a war in society that is as destructive to its weaker members as the custom of exposing the deformed and crippled children. Secondly—That slavery protects the weaker members of society just as do the relations of parent, guardian and husband, and is as necessary, as natural, and almost as universal as those relations. Is our demonstration imperfect? Does universal experience sustain our theory? Should the conclusions to which we have arrived appear strange and startling, let them therefore not be rejected without examination. The world has had but little opportunity to contrast the working of Liberty and Equality with the old order of things, which always partook more or less of the character of domestic slavery. The strong prepossession in the public mind in favor of the new system, makes it reluctant to attribute the evil phenomena which it exhibits, to defects inherent in the system itself. That these defects should not have been foreseen and pointed out by any process of *a priori* reasoning, is but another proof of the fallibility of human sagacity and foresight when attempting to foretell the operation of new institutions. It is as much as human reason can do, when examining the complex frame of society, to trace effects back to their causes—much more than it can do, to foresee what effects new causes will produce. We invite investigation.

HENRY HUGHES (1829-1862)

A TREATISE ON SOCIOLOGY.

NOMINALLY A LAWYER PRACTICING at Port Gibson, Mississippi, the precocious Henry Hughes seems to have spent much of his time among books, even though he was also moderately active in public life. His intense conviction that slavery was the most beneficent of all social systems led him, while serving in the state legislature, to agitate for the restoration of the African slave trade. He was a passionate Southern patriot; he enjoyed leaving his studies to drill with the local militia, and in the early months of the Civil War he commanded the 12th Mississippi regiment.

In 1854 Hughes, at the age of twenty-five, became the first American writer to use Auguste Comte's newly coined word "Sociology" in the title of a book. In his *Treatise on Sociology*, published that year, Hughes discerned a near-Utopian perfection in the South's labor arrangements, which he insisted on calling "Warranteeism" rather than "Slavery." Contrasted with free society, this marvelous balance among social, economic, and "hygienic" relationships was one in which all possible goods were "warranted."

The following selection consists of the two final chapters of the *Treatise*, intended by their author as a summary of the whole. The reader, after having accustomed himself to the pseudo-clinical prose style, will be struck and perhaps amused by the florid peroration that concludes the work. Dimly as the idea of "social science" was perceived 110 years ago, it already seemed to call for peculiarly synthetic language habits, and we may fancy that Hughes, having obeyed these unnatural coercions throughout his book, could not resist finishing off with a broad splash of purple.

CHAPTER XI.

SOCIETY IS AN ORGANIZATION, or an adaptation of means to ends. The first end is the existence of all. The second end is the progress of all. Systems compose organizations. Of a perfect societary organization, the components are perfect systems. These systems are the economic, the political, the hygienic, the ethical, the religious, the philosophic, and the esthetic. They are seven: each a necessary

A Treatise on Sociology, Theoretical and Practical (Philadelphia: Lippincott, Grambo & Co., 1854), pp. 286-92.

expedient to the ends of the societary organization. The perfection of this, is by the perfection of those.

The two forms of societary organization, are the free sovereign, and the ordered sovereign, or warranted. Each form is its performance. What therefore, is their comparative expediency? What is their comparative achievement? What is their comparative fulfilment of the ends of society? What is the comparative sociological condition of their systems? What is the comparative obtention, actualization, execution, performance, or realization of each form?

Warranteeism actualizes the first end of society, and is progressive. It achieves the healthy existence of all. To this, three warranted or ordered systems are necessary. These are the Political, the Economic, and the Hygienic. Warranteeism realizes them. In these systems, power and order are warranted. Order is public. It is ordained and established. Necessary association, adaptation and regulation are instituted. They are not accidental: they are essential.

In the economic system, production is orderly. Systematic quantitative adaptation of laborers and capital, is warranted. Laborers are adaptable. They are associated. They are regular. Economic irregularities are eliminated or accidental. Laborers never want work. If they do; provision for its supply is warranted. The laborer is appreciated. He is a material product. His aggregate and local production, and the values therefrom; are warranted. Strikes and idleness are eliminated. Capitalists can procure laborers; and laborers, capitalists. Laborers are never out of employment. If there is no demand; they are circulated to the place of demand. They are adscripts of capital. The productive department of the economic system, is in its essentials, perfect.

In the distribution of the warrantee economy, the distributor is the State or function of justice. Wages are warranted. Their quantity is essentially just. They continue for life, during both efficiency and inefficiency. Wages are variable, but these variations are never below the standard of comfortable sufficiency of necessaries. Want is eliminated. There are no poor: all have competence.

In the department of consumption, consumables sufficient for the reproduction of all are warranted. Every laborer has a sufficient supply of consumables. There is neither consumptive nor unproductive waste. Consumption is associate and regular. Laborers are not consumed: they are preserved: they are treasured. The preservation is by preservation-interest, intelligence, and capital. Capital is supplied for the laborers' preservation. The capitalists' preservation-interest in the laborer is warranted. Capital and labor, are syntagonistic. A laborer does not divide his subsistence with wife and children. This is needless. The subsistence of all is warranted to all.

The hygienic system of warranteeism is so methodized, that hygienic necessaries are warranted. Hygienic power and order, are warranted. This system is both preventive and curative.

Amalgamation of races is systematically suppressed. Caste for the purity and progress of races, is actualized. The purity of the females of one race, is systematically preserved. Association adaptable to the execution of hygienic rules, is established.

In the warrantee political system, justice and expediency are actualized. Injustice is accidental. It is eliminated by progress. All have substantially their rights. The sovereignty of one race, and the subsovereignty of the other, are morally commanded. This command is executed.

The maximum of civil power, wisdom and goodness, is realized. All of one race, are thinkers. This, by their vocation. They are mentalists. Crime from economic causes, is eliminated. The fundamental laws for the public peace, public health, public industry and public subsistence, are executed. The executive department combines the greatest number of magistrates, with the greatest desire, and the greatest ability. In the legislative department, all are represented; and the representation is efficient.

CHAPTER XII.

In the economic system of the Free-labor form of societary organization, order is not ordained and established. Association, adaptation, and regulation are free. They are not essential; they are accidental. They are not fundamental. They are not publicly instituted. The relation of capitalist and laborer, or of master and servant, is private. Their interests are not syntagonistic.

Systematic quantitative adaptation of laborers and capital, is not actualized. Laborers are not appreciated. They have not the value produced by circulation; the value of local production from where they are not in demand to where they are. To the capitalists, superficiency or excess of laborers, is desirable; because more than a sufficiency, is more orderly.

Distribution is not by the function of justice or the State. It is accidental. The distributor may be either the capitalist or the laborer. Their interests are antagonistic. Their antagonisms are not equipollent. Injustice is actualized. Wages may vary below the standard of comfortable sufficiency. Inefficients are not warranted subsistence. None are warranted. Want is not eliminated. Wages are variable to unhealthy, criminal, and mortal want. The young, the old, and other inefficients are supported not by the capital of capitalists, but by the wages of the laborers. The amount of these wages, is not adapted to the amount of the consumers; there is no discrimination. Pauperism is not eliminated.

The consumption of laborers is not the least possible. The capitalist has no preservation-interest in the laborer. Loss of a laborer is not the capitalist's loss.

Subsistence is not warranted to the laborers; neither is work or the means of subsistence.

In the Free-labor hygienic system, hygienic necessaries are not an element of laborers' wages. Capital is not supplied for the production of his health. The capitalist is not hygienically syntagonistic. Medicine, medical attendance, nursing, and therapeutical necessaries, are not warranted to laborers. They are not treasured. Their sickness or death, is not a direct economic injury to the capitalist.

In the Free-labor political system, the interests of classes are not syntagonistic. Taxes are not an element of wages paid by the capitalist: Crime from economic causes, is not eliminated. There are no economic methods, for the prevention of offences. There are no economic general and special securities. The magistracy are expensive and political only. The rich and poor, conflict. Agrarianism is not eliminated. The fundamental laws for the public health, public peace, public industry and public subsistence, are not executed. The interest is deficient, and the order. Strikes and riots are not eliminated. The expediencies of the political system, are political only; the economic system is not civilly. ordained and established. It is not a civil implement.

Both Free-labor and Warrantee forms of society, are progressive. Free-labor progress is a progress by antagonisms. Warrantee progress is a progress by syntagonisms. The Free-labor form of society, must be abolished; it must progress to the form of mutual-insurance or warranteeism. It must progress from immunity to community. It must necessitate association. It must warrant the existence and progress of all. Men must not be free-laborers; they must be LIBERTY-LABORERS. LIBERTY-LABOR MUST BE THE SUBSTITUTR of FREE-LABOR. That must be abolished. But the abolition must not be sudden, or disorderly. It must not be that kind of abolition, which is mere destruction. It must be canonical. It must be humane, just, truthful, pure, and orderly; the envelopment of the evil, by the development of the good.

The economic system in the United States South, is not slavery. IT IS WARRANTEEISM WITH THE ETHNICAL QUALIFICATION. It is just. It is expedient. It is progressive. It does not progress by antagonisms. It progresses by syntagonisms. It is in no way slavery. Religiously, it is Ebedism; economically, Warranteeism. The consummation of its progress, is the perfection of society.

And when in other generations, this progress, which is now a conception and a hope of all, shall be a memory and a fact; when what is now in the future, shall be in the present or the past; when the budding poetry of the all-hoping sociologist, shall ripen to a fruitful history; that history will be thrice felicitous; for it shall unroll the trophied poem, the rhapsody of a progress epic in its grandeur; pastoral in its peace; and lyric in its harmony. Such shall be its fulfilment. And then on leagued plantations over the sun-sceptred zone's crop-jeweled length, myriad eyes, both night-faced and morning-cheeked, shall brighten still the patriot's student glance and fondly pore upon the full-grown and fate-favored wonder, of a Federal banner in whose woven sky of ensign orbs, shall be good stars only, in such happy constellations that their bonds and beams, will be sweeter than the sweet influences of the Pleiades, and stronger than the bands of Orion; unbroken constel-

lations—a symbol sky—a heaven which also, shall declare the glory
of God, and a firmament which shall show His handiwork. Then,
in the plump flush of full-feeding health, the happy warrantees
shall banquet in PLANTATION-REFECTORIES; worship in PLANTATION-
CHAPELS; learn in PLANTATION-SCHOOLS; or, in PLANTATION-SALOONS,
at the cool of evening, or in the green and bloomy gloom of cold
catalpas and magnolias, chant old songs, tell tales; or, to the metred
rattle of chattering castanets, or flutes, or rumbling tamborines,
dance down the moon and evening star; and after slumbers in
PLANTATION-DORMITORIES, over whose gates Health and Rest sit
smiling at the feet of Wealth and Labor, rise at the music-crowing
of the morning-conchs, to begin again welcome days of jocund toil,
in reeling fields, where, weak with laughter and her load, Plenty
yearly falls, gives up, and splits her o'erstuffed horn, and where
behind twin Interest's double throne, Justice stands at reckoning
dusk, and rules supreme. When these and more than these, shall
be the fulfilment of Warranteeism; then shall this Federation and
the World, praise the power, wisdom, and goodness of a system,
which may well be deemed divine; then shall Experience aid Philosophy, and VINDICATE THE WAYS OF GOD, TO MAN.

WILLIAM J. GRAYSON (1788-1863)

THE HIRELING AND THE SLAVE.

OF THE VARIOUS SOUTHERN WRITERS who lent their energies to the defense of slavery in the 1850s, one of the most attractive was William Grayson, an elderly gentleman of South Carolina. Grayson had had a long career of public service which included terms in the state legislature and the Federal Congress; later, during the administrations of Tyler, Polk, and Fillmore, he was Collector of the Port of Charleston. He was a prosperous planter, a cultivated amateur of letters, and member of a circle which included Simms, Legaré, Petigru, Timrod, and Hayne. In politics he opposed the Calhoun party, and in the fifties he and his friend Petigru spoke earnestly against the growing disunionism of other South Carolina leaders. At the end, however, Grayson, like most Southern moderates, "went with his state."

Being of conservative temperament, Grayson was deeply pained by what he regarded as the unseemly agitation of both the English and American abolitionists. In 1856 he published a very long poem in heroic couplets, *The Hireling and the Slave*, devoted to a theme already familiar in pro-slavery polemics: the immense advantages enjoyed by the transplanted African slave compared with the bitter lot of the "free" worker who toiled for a bare subsistence. But unlike Fitzhugh and Hammond, for whom these exploited workers abounded on both sides of the Atlantic, Grayson preferred to restrict his "wage slaves" to England and Europe.

A portion of the poem follows.

> FALLEN FROM PRIMEVAL innocence and ease,
> When thornless fields employed him but to please,
> The laborer toils; and from his dripping brow
> Moistens the length'ning furrows of the plow;
> In vain he scorns or spurns his altered state,
> Tries each poor shift, and strives to cheat his fate;
> In vain new-shapes his name to shun the ill—
> Slave, hireling, help—the curse pursues him still;
> Changeless the doom remains, the mincing phrase

The Hireling and the Slave, Chicora, and Other Poems (Charleston: McCord & Co., 1856), pp. 21-45, *passim*.

May mock high Heaven, but not reverse its ways.
How small the choice, from cradle to the grave,
Between the lot of hireling, help, or slave!
To each alike applies the stern decree
That man shall labor; whether bond or free,
For all that toil, the recompense we claim—
Food, fire, a home and clothing—is the same.

   The manumitted serfs of Europe find
Unchanged this sad estate of all mankind;
What blessing to the churl has freedom proved,
What want supplied, what task or toil removed?
Hard work and scanty wages still their lot,
In youth o'erlabored, and in age forgot,
The mocking boon of freedom they deplore,
In wants and labors never known before.*

   Free but in name—the slaves of endless toil,
In Britain still they turn the stubborn soil,
Spread on each sea her sails for every mart,
Ply in her cities every useful art;
But vainly may the peasant toil and groan
To speed the plow in furrows not his own;
In vain the art is plied, the sail is spread,
The day's work offered for the daily bread;
With hopeless eye, the pauper hireling sees
The homeward sail swell proudly to the breeze,
Rich fabrics wrought by his unequaled hand,
Borne by each breeze to every distant land;
For him, no boon successful commerce yields,
For him no harvest crowns the joyous fields,
The streams of wealth that foster pomp and pride,
No food nor shelter for his wants provide;
He fails to win, by toil intensely hard,
The bare subsistence—labor's least reward.

   In squalid hut—a kennel for the poor,
Or noisome cellar, stretched upon the floor,

---

* Pauperism began with the abolition of serfage.—*Westminster Review.*

His clothing rags, of filthy straw his bed,
With offal from the gutter daily fed,
Thrust out from Nature's board, the hireling lies:
No place for him that common board supplies,
No neighbor helps, no charity attends,
No philanthropic sympathy befriends;
None heed the needy wretch's dying groan,
He starves unsuccor'd, perishes unknown.
    These are the miseries, such the wants, the cares,
The bliss that freedom for the serf prepares;
Vain is his skill in each familiar task,
Capricious Fashion shifts her Protean mask,
His ancient craft gives work and bread no more,
And Want and Death sit scowling at his door.
    Close by the hovel, with benignant air,
To lordly halls illustrious crowds repair*—
The Levite tribes of Christian love that show
No care nor pity for a neighbor's woe;
Who meet, each distant evil to deplore,
But not to clothe or feed their country's poor;
They waste no thought on common wants or pains,
On misery hid in filthy courts and lanes,
On alms that ask no witnesses but Heaven,
By pious hands to secret suffering given;
Theirs the bright sunshine of the public eye,
The pomp and circumstance of charity,
The crowded meeting, the repeated cheer,
The sweet applause of prelate, prince, or peer,
The long report of pious trophies won
Beyond the rising or the setting sun,
The mutual smile, the self-complacent air,
The labored speech and Pharisaic prayer,
Thanksgivings for their purer hearts and hands,
Scorn for the publicans of other lands,
And soft addresses—Sutherland's delight,

* Exeter Hall, the show-place of English philanthropy.

That gentle dames at pious parties write—
These are the cheats that vanity prepares,
The charmed deceits of her seductive fairs,
When Exeter expands her portals wide,
And England's saintly coteries decide
The proper nostrum for each evil known
In every land on earth, except their own,
But never heed the sufferings, wants, or sins
At home, where all true charity begins.

There, unconcerned, the philanthropic eye
Beholds each phase of human misery;
Sees the worn child compelled in mines to slave
Through narrow seams of coal, a living grave,
Driven from the breezy hill, the sunny glade,
By ruthless hearts, the drudge of labor made,
Unknown the boyish sport, the hours of play,
Stripped of the common boon, the light of day,
Harnessed like brutes, like brutes to tug, and strain,
And drag, on hands and knees, the loaded wain:
There crammed in huts, in reeking masses thrown,
All moral sense and decency unknown,
With no restraint but what the felon knows,
With the sole joy that beer or gin bestows,
To gross excess and brutalizing strife,
The drunken hireling dedicates his life:
Starved else, by infamy's sad wages fed,
There women prostitute themselves for bread,
And mothers, rioting with savage glee,
For murder'd infants spend the funeral fee;
Childhood bestows no childish sports or toys,
Age neither reverence nor repose enjoys,
Labor with hunger wages ceaseless strife,
And want and suffering only end with life;
In crowded huts contagious ills prevail,
Dull typhus lurks, and deadlier plagues assail,
Gaunt Famine prowls around his pauper prey,
And daily sweeps his ghastly hosts away;

Unburied corses taint the summer air,
And crime and outrage revel with despair.

        .   .   .   .   .   .

Yet homebred misery, such as this, imparts
Nor grief nor care to philanthropic hearts;
The tear of sympathy forever flows,
Though not for Saxon or for Celtic woes;
Vainly the starving white, at every door,
Craves help or pity for the hireling poor;
But that the distant black may softlier fare,
Eat, sleep, and play, exempt from toil and care,
All England's meek philanthropists unite
With frantic eagerness, harangue and write;
By purchased tools diffuse distrust and hate,
Sow factious strife in each dependent state,
Cheat with delusive lies the public mind,
Invent the cruelties they fail to find,
Slander, in pious garb, with prayer and hymn,
And blast a people's fortune for a whim.
Cursed by these factious arts, that take the guise
Of charity to cheat the good and wise,
The bright Antilles, with each closing year,
See harvests fail, and fortunes disappear;
The cane no more its golden treasure yields;
Unsightly weeds deform the fertile fields;
The negro freeman, thrifty while a slave,
Loosed from restraint, becomes a drone or knave;
Each effort to improve his nature foils,
Begs, steals, or sleeps and starves, but never toils;
For savage sloth mistakes the freedom won,
And ends the mere barbarian he begun.
Then, with a face of self-complacent smiles,
Pleased with the ruin of these hapless isles,
And charmed with this cheap way of gaining heaven
By alms at cost of other countries given—
Like Nathan's host, who hospitably gave

His guest a neghbor's lamb his own to save,
Clarkson's meek school beholds with eager eyes,
In other climes, new fields of glory rise,
And heedless still of home, its care bestows,
In other lands, on other Negro woes.

Hesperian lands, beyond the Atlantic wave,
Home of the poor, and refuge of the brave,
Who, vainly striving with oppression, fly
To find new homes beneath a happier sky;
Hither, to quiet vale or mountain side,
Where Peace and Nature undisturbed abide,
In humble scenes unwonted lore to learn,
Patriot and prince their banished footsteps turn;
The exiled Bourbon finds a place of rest,
And Kossuth comes, a nation's thankless guest;
Here, driven by bigots to their last retreat,
All forms of faith a safe asylum meet,
Each as it wills, untouched by former fears,
Its prayer repeats, its cherished altar rears. . . .
Here, with determined will and patient toil,
From wood and swamp he wins the fertile soil;
To every hardship stern endurance brings,
And builds a fortune undisturbed by kings;
Fair fields of wealth and ease his children find,
Nor heed the homes their fathers left behind.

Companions of his toil, the axe to wield,
To guide the plow, and reap the teeming field,
A sable multitude unceasing pour
From Niger's banks and Congo's deadly shore;
No willing travelers they, that widely roam,
Allured by hope to seek a happier home,
But victims to the trader's thirst for gold,
Kidnapped by brothers, and by fathers sold,
The bondsman born, by native masters reared,
The captive band in recent battle spared;
For English merchants bought; across the main,

In British ships, they go for Britain's gain;
Forced on her subjects in dependent lands,
By cruel hearts and avaricious hands,
New tasks they learn, new masters they obey,
And bow submissive to the white man's sway.
   But Providence, by his o'erruling will,
Transmutes to lasting good the transient ill,
Makes crime itself the means of mercy prove,
And avarice minister to works of love.
In this new home, whate'er the negro's fate—
More bless'd his life than in his native state!
No mummeries dupe, no Fetich charms affright,
Nor rites obscene diffuse their moral blight;
Idolatries, more hateful than the grave,
With human sacrifice, no more enslave;
No savage rule its hecatomb supplies
Of slaves for slaughter when a master dies:
In sloth and error sunk for countless years
His race has lived, but light at last appears—
Celestial light: religion undefiled
Dawns in the heart of Congo's simple child;
Her glorious truths he hears with glad surprise,
And lifts his eye with rapture to the skies;
The noblest thoughts that erring mortals know,
Waked by her influence, in his bosom glow;
His nature owns the renovating sway,
And all the old barbarian melts away.
   And now, with sturdy hand and cheerful heart,
He learns to master every useful art,
To forge the axe, to mould the rugged share,
The ship's brave keel for angry waves prepare:
The rising wall obeys his plastic will,
And the loom's fabric owns his ready skill.
   Where once the Indian's keen, unerring aim,
With shafts of reed transfixed the forest game,
Where painted warriors late in ambush stood,

And midnight war-whoops shook the trembling wood,
The Negro wins, with well-directed toil,
Its various treasures from the virgin soil.

    .   .   .   .   .

These precious products, in successive years,
Trained by a master's skill, the Negro rears;
New life he gives to Europe's busy marts,
To all the world new comforts and new arts;
Loom, spinner, merchant, from his hands derive
Their wealth, and myriads by his labor thrive;
While slothful millions, hopeless of relief,
The slaves of pagan priest and brutal chief,
Harassed by wars upon their native shore,
Still lead the savage life they led before.
Instructed thus, and in the only school
Barbarians ever know—a master's rule,
The Negro learns each civilizing art
That softens and subdues the savage heart,
Assumes the tone of those with whom he lives,
Acquires the habit that refinement gives,
And slowly learns, but surely, while a slave,
The lessons that his country never gave.

    .   .   .   .

Hence is the Negro come, by God's command,
For wiser teaching to a foreign land;
If they who brought him were by Mammon driven,
Still have they served, blind instruments of Heaven;
And though the way be rough, the agent stern,
No better mode can human wits discern,
No happier system wealth or virtue find,
To tame and elevate the Negro mind:
Thus mortal purposes, whate'er their mood,
Are only means with Heaven for working good;
And wisest they who labor to fulfill,

With zeal and hope, the all-directing will,
And in each change that marks the fleeting year,
Submissive see God's guiding hand appear.

.   .   .   .   .

But if, though wise and good the purposed end,
Reproach and scorn the instrument attend;
If, when the final blessing is confess'd,
Still the vile slaver all the world detest;
Arraign the states that sent their ships of late
To barter beads and rum for human freight,
That claimed the right, by treaty, to provide
Slaves for themselves, and half the world beside,
And from the Hebrew learned the craft so well,
Their sable brothers to enslave and sell.
Shame and remorse o'erwhelmed the Hebrew race,
And penitence was stamped on every face;
But modern slavers, more sagacious grown,
In all the wrong, can see no part their own;
They drag the Negro from his native shore,
Make him a slave, and then his fate deplore;
Sell him in distant countries, and when sold,
Revile the buyers, but retain the gold:
Dext'rous to win, in time, by various ways,
Substantial profit and alluring praise,
By turns they grow rapacious and humane,
And seize alike the honor and the gain:
Had Joseph's brethren known this modern art,
And played with skill the philanthropic part,
How had bold Judah raved in freedom's cause,
How Levi cursed the foul Egyptian laws,
And Issachar, in speech or long report,
Brayed at the masters found in Pharaoh's court,
And taught the king himself the sin to hold
Enslaved the brother they had lately sold.
Proving that sins of traffic never lie

On knaves who sell, but on the dupes that buy.
Such now the maxims of the purer school*
Of ethic lore, where sons of slavers rule;
No more allowed the Negro to enslave,
They damn the master, and for freedom rave,
Strange modes of morals and of faith unfold,
Make newer gospels supersede the old,
Prove that ungodly Paul connived at sin,
And holier rites, like Mormon's priest, begin. . . .
These use the Negro, a convenient tool,
That yields substantial gain or party rule,
Gives what without it they could never know,
To Chase distinction, courtly friends to Stowe,
To Parker, themes for miracles of rant,
And Beecher blesses with new gifts of cant.
The master's task has been the black to train,
To form his mind, his passions to restrain;
With anxious care and patience to impart
The knowledge that subdues the savage heart,
To give the Gospel lessons that control
The rudest breast, and renovate the soul—
Who does, or gives as much, of all who raise
Their sland'rous cry for foreign pence or praise;
Of all the knaves who clamor and declaim
For party power or philanthropic fame,
Or use the Negro's fancied wrongs and woes
As pretty themes for maudlin verse or prose?
Taught by the master's efforts, by his care
Fed, clothed, protected many a patient year,
From trivial numbers now to millions grown,
With all the white man's useful arts their own,
Industrious, docile, skilled in wood and field,
To guide the plow, the sturdy axe to wield,
The Negroes schooled by slavery embrace

---

* The purer school of New England, which sets aside the Constitution and
the Gospel, and substitutes Parker for St. Paul, and Beecher and Garrison for
the Evangelists.

The highest portion of the Negro race;
And none the savage native will compare,
Of barbarous Guinea, with its offspring here.
  If bound to daily labor while he lives,
His is the daily bread that labor gives;
Guarded from want, from beggary secure,
He never feels what hireling crowds endure,
Nor knows, like them, in hopeless want to crave,
For wife and child, the comforts of the slave,
Or the sad thought that, when about to die,
He leaves them to the cold world's charity,
And sees them slowly seek the poor-house door—
The last, vile, hated refuge of the poor.
  Still Europe's saints, that mark the motes alone
In other's eyes, yet never see their own,
Grieve that the slave is never taught to write,
And reads no better than the hireling white;
Do their own plowmen no instruction lack,
Have whiter clowns more knowledge than the black?
Has the French peasant, or the German boor,
Of learning's treasure any larger store;
Have Ireland's millions, flying from the rule
Of those who censure, ever known a school?
A thousand years and Europe's wealth impart
No means to mend the hireling's head or heart;
They build no schools to teach the pauper white,
Their toiling millions neither read nor write;
Whence, then, the idle clamor when they rave
Of schools and teachers for the distant slave?
  And why the soft regret, the coarse attack,
If Justice punish the offending black?
Are whites not punished? When Utopian times
Shall drive from earth all miseries and crimes,
And teach the world the art to do without
The cat, the gauntlet, and the brutal knout,
Banish the halter, galley, jails, and chains,
And strip the law of penalties and pains:

Here, too, offense and wrong they may prevent,
And slaves, with hirelings, need no punishment:
Till then, what lash of slavery will compare
With the dread scourge that British soldiers bear?
What gentle rule, in Britain's Isle, prevails,
How rare her use of gibbets, stocks, and jails!
How much humaner than a master's whip,
Her penal colony and convict ship!
Whose code of law can darker pages show,
Where blood for smaller misdemeanors flow?
The trifling theft or trespass, that demands
For slaves light penance from a master's hands,
Where Europe's milder punishments are known,
Incurs the penalty of death alone.

    And yet the master's lighter rule insures
More order than the sternest code secures;
No mobs of factious workmen gather here,
No strikes we dread, no lawless riots fear;
Nuns, from their convent driven, at midnight fly,
Churches, in flames, ask vengeance from the sky,
Seditious schemes in bloody tumults end,
Parsons incite, and senators defend,
But not where slaves their easy labors ply,
Safe from the snare, beneath a master's eye;
In useful tasks engaged, employed their time,
Untempted by the demagogue to crime,
Secure they toil, uncursed their peaceful life, `
With labor's hungry broils and wasteful strife.
No want to goad, no faction to deplore, `
The slave escapes the perils of the poor.

      .   .   .   .   .

EDMUND RUFFIN (1794-1865)

THE POLITICAL ECONOMY
OF SLAVERY.

In the history of the ante-bellum South Edmund Ruffin became famous in each of three separate capacities—as a scientific agriculturist, as a fanatical secessionist, and as a fluent defender of slavery. His experiments in soil restoration with calcareous earths won him distinction both in and outside his native state of Virginia. He was an early disunionist; he was given the honor of firing the first shot against Fort Sumter, and when the Confederacy collapsed in 1865 the aged Yankee-hater seized a pistol and blew out his brains.

Ruffin's writings on slavery appeared in many of the South's leading newspapers and periodicals and were published in pamphlet form as well; coming as they did from a man of his influence they were received with much respect. His *Political Economy of Slavery*, published in 1853, shows the influence of several varieties of the pro-slavery argument, including the work of George Fitzhugh. The reader may wish to judge, in the following excerpt, the extent to which the author succeeds in reconciling two apparently inconsistent positions. Ruffin argues, on the one hand, that slave labor is in the long run cheaper than free labor; the blessings of slavery for the slave, on the other hand, are presumably owing to the added burdens and responsibilities which the master assumes in caring for him—responsibilities which the greedy capitalist employer, concerned only for profit, evades.

SLAVERY GENERAL IN ANCIENT TIMES—CAUSES OF SLAVERY—
AVERSION TO LABOR OF DEGRADED CLASSES
AND OF BARBAROUS COMMUNITIES.

SLAVERY HAS EXISTED from as early time as historical records furnish any information of the social and political condition of mankind. There was no country, in the most ancient time of its history, of which the people had made any considerable advances in industry

The Political Economy of Slavery; or, The Institution Considered in Regard to Its Influence on Public Wealth and the General Welfare (Washington: Lemuel Towers, 1853), n. p.

or refinement, in which slavery had not been previously and long established, and in general use. The reasons for this universal early existence of slavery, and of domestic or individual slavery, (except among the most ignorant and savage tribes,) can be readily deduced from the early conditions of society.

Whether in savage or civilized life, the lower that individuals are degraded by poverty and want, and the fewer are their means for comfort, and the enjoyment of either intellectual or physical pleasures, or of relief from physical sufferings, the lower do they descend in their appreciation of actual and even natural wants; and the more do they magnify and dread the efforts and labors necessary to protect themselves against the occurrence of the privations and sufferings with which they are threatened. When man sinks so low as not to feel artificial wants, or utterly to despair of gratifying any such wants, he becomes brutishly careless and indolent, even in providing for natural and physical wants, upon which provision even life is dependent. All such persons soon learn to regard present and continuous labor as an evil greater than the probable but uncertain future occurrence of extreme privation, or even famine, and consequent death from want. Hence the most savage tribes of tropical regions are content to rely for sustenance almost entirely on the natural productions of a fertile and bounteous soil. The savage inhabitants of less fruitful lands, and under more rigorous climates, depend on hunting and fishing for a precarious support, and with irregular alternations of abundance and lavish waste, with destitution and hunger and famine. . . . Even in countries, and among a general population, in which the highest rewards are held out for labor and industry—where some intellectual, and also moral and religious instruction, are within the reach of all who will seek and accept such benefits, there are numerous cases of men who not only forego all intellectual and moral improvement for themselves and their families, and the attempt to gratify all artificial wants, but who also neglect the relief of the most humble comforts and even necessaries of life, rather than resort to that regular course of labor which would furnish the means for comfortable subsistence. In all such cases—whether in civilized or in savage society, or whether in regard to individuals, families in successive generations, or to more extended communities—a good and proper remedy for this evil, if it could be applied, would be the enslaving of these reckless, wretched drones and cumberers of the earth, and thereby compelling them to habits of labor, and in return satisfying their wants for necessaries, and raising them and their progeny in the scale of humanity, not only physically, but morally and intellectually. Such a measure would be the most beneficial in young and rude communities, where labor is scarce and dear, and the means for subsistence easy to obtain. For even among a barbarous people, where the aversion to labor is universal, those who could not be induced to labor with their own hands, and in person, if they became slaveholders, would be ready enough to compel the labor of their slaves, and also would soon learn to economize and accumulate the products of their labor. Hence, among any savage people, the introduction and establishment of domestic slavery is necessarily an improvement of the condition and wealth and well-being of the community in general, and also of the comfort of the enslaved class, if it had consisted of such persons as were lowest in the social scale —and is beneficial in every such case to the master class, and to the community in general.

INDOLENCE OF FREE LABORERS AT HIGH WAGES—DIFFERENT INCENTIVES TO FREE AND SLAVE LABOR—COMPARATIVE VALUES.

But the disposition to indulge indolence (even at great sacrifices of benefit which might be secured by industrious labor) is not peculiar to the lowest and most degraded classes of civilized communities. It is notorious that, whenever the demand for labor is much greater than the supply, or the wages of labor are much higher than the expenses of living, very many, even of the ordinary laboring class, are remarkable for indolence, and work no more than compelled by necessity. The greater the demand, and the higher the rewards, for labor, the less will be performed, as a general rule, by each individual laborer. If the wages of work for one day will support the laborer or mechanic and his family for three, it will be very likely that he will be idle two-thirds of his time.

Slave labor, in each individual case, and for each small measure of time, is more slow and inefficient than the labor of a free man.

The latter knows that the more work he performs in a short time, the greater will be his reward in earnings. Hence, he has every inducement to exert himself while at work for himself, even though he may be idle for a longer time afterwards. The slave receives the same support, in food, clothing, and other allowances, whether he works much or little; and hence he has every inducement to spare himself as much as possible, and to do as little work as he can, without drawing on himself punishment, which is the only incentive to slave labor. It is, then, an unquestionable general truth, that the labor of a free man, for any stated time, is more than the labor of a slave, and if at the same cost, would be cheaper to the employer. Hence it has been inferred, and asserted by all who argue against slavery, and is often admitted even by those who would defend its expediency, that, as a general rule, and for whole communities, free labor is cheaper than slave labor. The rule is false, and the exceptions only are true. Suppose it admitted that the labor of slaves, for each hour or day, will amount to but two-thirds of what hired free laborers would perform in the same time. But the slave labor is continuous, and every day at least it returns to the employers and to the community, this two-thirds of full labor. Free laborers, if to be hired for the like duties, would require at least double the amount of wages to perform one-third more labor in each day, and in general, would be idle and earning nothing, more length of time than that spent in labor. Then, on these premises and suppositions, it is manifest that slave labor, with its admitted defect in this respect, will be cheapest and most profitable to the employer, and to the whole community, and will yield more towards the general increase of production and public wealth; and that the free laborer who is idle two days out of three, even if receiving double wages for his days of labor, is less laborious, and less productive for himself, and for the community, and the public wealth, than the slave.

The mistake of those who maintain, or admit, this generally asserted proposition, that "free labor is cheaper than slave labor", is caused by assuming as true, that self-interest induces free hirelings to labor continuously and regularly. This is never the case in general, except where daily and continuous labor is required to obtain a bare daily subsistence. That case, and its consequences, will be considered hereafter. For the present, I will return to the causes of slavery.

WAR FORMERLY A SOURCE AND PRODUCER OF SLAVERY.

Though slavery would, in the manner above stated, have been introduced (if not otherwise) among every savage people above the lowest and least improvable condition of the savage state, still the institution generally preceded, and so prevented, the existence of these conditions. For there were other still earlier and sufficiently operative causes. As soon as men outgrew and emerged from strictly patriarchal or pure family government, (the most ancient of all) and were included in larger communities, under governments of usurpation and force, it must be supposed, that the strong ruled and oppressed the weak, whether acting or acted upon as individuals or as communities, and in that manner that the weaker would become slaves to the stronger. If not produced otherwise, this would necessarily be the result of war between semi-barbarous communities; and war has existed between such communities, and has rarely ceased, since men were first arrayed in different political bodies. Where civilization and refinement were so low as among the most ignorant savages of Australia, or most of the North American Indians, the prisoners of war would be put to death, because no profitable use could be made of them. But where any advances had been made in regular industry, and especially where the right of private property in land had been established, the expediency of making domestic slaves and laborers of prisoners of war would soon be acknowledged and acted upon. Thus one of the earliest effects of the institution of slavery would be to lessen the horrors of war by saving lives that would otherwise be sacrificed.

SLAVERY IMPOSED AS PENALTY FOR CRIME OR DEBT.

In the early conditions of society and of private property, most of the debtors to individuals, or to the sovereign, or delinquents whose punishments were pecuniary or property amercements, would rarely have any other property or means for payment than their own persons. Hence would certainly follow (as still is the usage in barbarous countries) slavery as the payment for debt, and penalty for crimes, or offences against the sovereign or the laws. With the injustice and cruelty usual in all barbarous communities, the families of delinquents thus condemned to slavery would also be enslaved. And if this were not ordered by vengeance and cruelty, it would almost surely be required by expediency, and even humanity. For the destitute wife and young children of a slave, and any future and more helpless infants, would generally need to be supported, or would perish from want. In barbarous communities, regular maintenance in such cases can only be had from a master who can afford to support infant and then unprofitable slaves, to be compensated by the subsequent labors of their mature life and profitable service. Thus, slavery would necessarily, and from the beginning, become hereditary, and be everywhere a permanent and fixed condition.

WHERE PERSONAL SLAVERY IS NOT NEEDED, AND IF PREVIOUSLY ESTABLISHED WOULD CEASE TO EXIST.

By the two modes above stated, slavery would necessarily be established in the early state of society of every young and barbarous community which was not so savage as to be destitute of all regular industry, and of the artificial wants which induce a demand for, or the desire to possess, the accumulated products of labor. Without the existence of such a demand for the services of slaves as will induce and compensate the providing for their regular and sufficient support, domestic slavery cannot be begun. And if before existing, neither can it be continued in old countries densely peopled, where the support of a slave will be more costly than the hire of a free man, driven to his greatest exertion by extreme want, and depressed by the competition of his fellows to the lowest rate of wages at which subsistence is possible.

THE EVILS AND BENEFITS OF SLAVERY STATED GENERALLY.

Slavery, when thus introduced, would be frequently attended with circumstances of great hardship, injustice, and sometimes atrocious cruelty. Still, the consequences and general results were highly beneficial. By this means only—the compulsion of domestic slaves —in the early conditions of society, could labor be made to produce

wealth. By this aid only could leisure be afforded to the master
class to cultivate mental improvement and refinement of manners;
and artificial wants be created and indulged, which would stimulate
the desire and produce the effect, to accumulate the products of
labor, which alone constitute private and public wealth. To the
operation and first results of domestic slavery were due the gradual
civilization and general improvement of manners and of arts among
all originally barbarous peoples, who, of themselves, or without
being conquered and subjugated (or enslaved politically) by a more
enlightened people, have subsequently emerged from barbarism and
dark ignorance. The slavery supposed to be thus introduced would
be the subjection of people of the same race with their masters—of
equals to equals—and therefore this would be slavery of the most
objectionable kind. It would involve most injustice and hardship to
the enslaved—would render it more difficult for the masters to command and enforce obedience—and would make the bonds of servitude more galling to the slaves, because of their being equal to their
masters (and, in many individual cases, greatly superior,) in natural
endowments of mind.

THE GREATEST WORKS OF ANCIENT NATIONS DUE TO SLAVERY, AND IN ITS WORST FORM.

Still, even this worst and least profitable kind of slavery (the
subjection of equals and men of the same race with their masters)
served as the foundation and the essential first cause of all the
civilization and refinement, and improvement of arts and learning,
that distinguished the oldest nations. Except where the special
Providence and care of God may have interposed to guard a particular family and its descendants, there was nothing but the existence
of slavery to prevent any race or society in a state of nature from
sinking into the rudest barbarism. And no people could ever have
been raised from that low condition without the aid and operation
of slavery, either by some individuals of the community being made
slaves to others, or the whole community being enslaved, by con-
quest and subjugation, in some form, to a foreign and more enlightened people. The very ancient and wonderful works of con-
struction and sculpture in Egypt and Hindostan could never have

been executed, nor even the desire to possess them conceived, except
where compulsory labor had long been in use, and could be applied
to such great works. And to the same cause was due, not only the
later and far more perfect and admirable works of art in Greece
and Rome, but also the marvellous triumphs of intellect among
these successive masters of the then known world. And not only
were great works of utility and ornament so produced, nations enriched and strengthened, and empires established and maintained,
but also there were moral results in private and social life, of far
more value. In much earlier time, it was on this institution of domestic slavery that was erected the admirable and benificent master-
ship and government of the patriarch Abraham, who owned so many
domestic slaves that he could suddenly call out and lead three
hundred and eighteen of them, able to bear arms, to repel and
punish the invasion of foreign hostile tribes. The like system of
domestic slavery then, and for many ages after, subsisted in every
part of the world in which any considerable moral or mental progress or economical improvement was to be seen. . . .

THE EXTINCTION OF INDIVIDUAL SLAVERY THE NECESSARY RESULT
OF AN EXCESS OF FREE LABOR—THE COMPETITION OF FREE
LABORERS, AND THEIR GREATEST SUFFERINGS, PRODUCE
THE GREATEST PROFITS OF CAPITAL.

But in every country, when covered by a dense population, and
when subsistence to free laborers becomes difficult to be obtained,
the competition for employment will tend to depress the price of
labor, gradually, to the lowest rate at which a bare subsistence can
be purchased. The indolence natural to man, and especially in his
lowest and most degraded state, can then no longer be indulged;
because to be idle would not be to suffer privation only, and to incur
risks of greater suffering, but absolutely and speedily to starve and
die of want. If domestic slavery could have continued to exist so
long, the slaves then would be in a very much better condition than
the free laborers, because possessing assured means for support, and
that for much less labor and hardship. For sharp want, hunger and
cold, are more effective incentives to labor than the slaveowner's

whip, even if its use is not restrained by any feeling of justice or mercy. But under such conditions of free labor, domestic or individual slavery could not exist. For whenever want and competition shall reduce the wages of free labor below the cost of slave labor, then it will be more profitable for the slaveowner and employer to hire free labor (both cheapened and driven by hunger and misery) than to maintain slaves, and compel their labor less effectually and at greater expense. Under such conditions, slaves (if they could not be sold and removed to some other country, where needed) would be readily emancipated by masters to whom they had become burdensome. Soon, under the operating influence of self-interest alone on the master class, domestic slavery would come to an end of itself —give place to the far more stringent and oppressive rule of want, as a compeller of labor, and be substituted by class-slavery, or the absolute subjection of the whole class of laborers to the whole class of employers—or labor to capital. Then, in the progress of society, first begins to be true, and soon becomes entirely true, the hackneyed proposition that "free labor is cheaper than slave labor"; and it is only true under these circumstances, when the supply of labor is regularly or generally greater than the demand. Then the surplus hands must be left without employment, and therefore without means for subsistence. They can obtain employment only by underbidding the rate of wages then received by the laborers employed, and so be engaged by throwing as many other laborers out of work. These must, in like manner, submit to the same reduction of wages, to be enabled again to obtain employment by getting the places of as many others. Finally, all are compelled to work for the reduced wages. But, after this general reduction, still, as before, the supply of hands will exceed (and more and more with the increase of population) the demand for their labor; as many therefore as are surplus must be always out of employment, and struggling to obtain it—and by the same process, competition, urged by extreme want, will tend still more to lower wages. Thus want and competition will continue to compel the superfluous and unemployed hands to submit to more and more reduction of wages, until the amount generally obtained is very much less than what is needed for the comfortable subsistence and healthy support of the laborer. And during all the time of this long continued competition and struggle for subsistence, while the rate of wages is being gradually lowered, the amount of toil of each laborer is increased—or at least as long as the human frame can bear increased exertion. *When the greatest possible amount of labor is thus obtained for the lowest amount of wages that can barely sustain life and strength for labor, there has been attained the most perfect and profitable condition of industrial operations for the class of capitalists and employers, and also for the most rapid increase of general and national wealth.* But these benefits (so much lauded and deemed so desirable for every country, and by almost every writer,) are purchased only by the greatest possible amount of toil, privation, and misery of the class of laborers under which they can live and work. It is readily admitted that slave labor could never yield anything like such large net returns— and that it would not only produce less, but would cost more. Slaves could not be subjected to such extreme privation and misery, be- cause they must be fed and clothed, and cannot generally be greatly over-worked, (and never to the profit of the master,) as is caused continually by the pressure of extreme want, and through competition, on free laborers. If the political and economical prob- lem to be worked out is the production of the greatest amount of profit to capitalists, and of wealth to the nation, in a country of dense population and advanced industrial operations, without regard to the sufferings of the laboring class, it is certain that the laborers must not be slaves, but free from all masters except extreme want. England, after the general abolition of slavery, was more than two centuries approaching this condition, which was finally reached, and has now been fully enjoyed for many years. Since then, England has been, of all the countries of the world, the most prosperous in manu- factures, commerce, and all industrial employments of capital and labor—and the laboring and poorest classes have been among the most destitute and miserable. That they have not been sunk, by competition for food, to still greater misery, and that many more numerous and frequent deaths have not occurred from absolute starvation, is owing to the introduction of another kind of slavery

—pauper slavery—which is the certain consequence of and the partial remedy for, the evils and sufferings produced by the competition of free labor. . . .

PAUPER SLAVERY.

. . . The pauper, whether laborer or otherwise, receiving support from the parish, is neither more nor less than a slave to the administrators of the law and dispensers of the public charity. The pauper ceases to be a free agent in any respect. If at work far from the place of his birth, (in England,) he is remanded and transported to his own or native parish, there to obtain support. If either this forced exile from his long previous place of residence and labor, or other reasons of expediency require it, husband and wife, and parents and children, are separated, and severally disposed of at the will of the overseers of the poor. The able-bodied laborer, who at his agricultural or other work can earn but six shillings a week, and cannot support his family for less than ten, may, indeed, obtain the deficient four shillings from the parish. But to do so, he is subject to be forced to take any service that the authorities may direct. And as the employer receives the pauper laborer against his will, and only because he thereby pays so much of his share of the poor-tax, he not only has the pauper as an involuntary slave, but he has not even the inducement of self-interest to treat the pauper slave well, or to care to preserve his health or life. The death of the pauper laborer is no loss to his temporary employer, and is a clear gain to the parish. Hence, while all of the millions of pauper population of England are truly slaves, and as much under constraint as if each one and his family belonged to an individual master, or as negro slaves are here, they have not the family comforts, or the care for the preservation of their health and lives, enjoyed by every negro slave in Virginia and Mississippi. The negro slaves in the United States have increased from 300,000, the number originally imported from Africa, to nearly 4,000,000, or more than twelve for one. This is a sufficient evidence of their general good treatment, induced by the self-interest of the owners. If it were possible to designate, separately, the whole class of poor laborers in England, and to trace them and their descendants for two hundred years, it is most probable that the original number would be found diminished in as great proportion as that in which our negro slaves have increased —or reduced to less than one-twelfth part. Yet this widespread, miserable, and life-destroying hunger slavery and pauper slavery in England is there called freedom by the fanatics and so-called philanthropists, who abhor, and call incessantly for God's vengeance upon, the negro slavery of this country! . . .

GENERAL AND EXTREME SUFFERING FROM WANT IMPOSSIBLE IN A SLAVEHOLDING COMMUNITY.

So long as domestic slavery is general in any country, and for the most part supplies the labor of the country, there is no possibility of the occurrence of the sufferings of the laboring class, such as were described above. There, the evils which are caused by extreme want and destitution, the competition for sustenance, class-slavery of labor to capital, and lastly pauper slavery, are all the incidents and necessary results of free society, and "free labor". Before such evils can visit any laboring class of personal slaves, they must have first been emancipated, and personal slavery abolished. This abolition of slavery is indeed like to occur in every country in the progress of society, and where the increasing population has no sufficient and advantageous outlet. But so long as domestic slavery remains, and is the main supply of labor, among any civilized people, it is a certain indication, and the most unquestionable evidence, that extensive and long continued suffering from want or hunger have as yet had no existence in that country. The first great effect of such distress will be to reduce (by competition) the wages of free labor below the cost of maintaining slaves—and this effect would next cause the extinction of slavery, by the mode of sale and exportation, or otherwise the emancipation of all the slaves. After this step has been made, of course, in due time, the want and suffering, which are the necessary incidents and consequences of free society, are to be expected to follow in after times.

When temporary evils, great loss, and distress, fall upon slaveholding countries, it is not the laboring class (as in free society) that feels the first and heaviest infliction, but the masters and employers. If a slaveholding country is visited by dearth, ravaged by war, or by pestilence—or suffers under any other causes of widespread calamity—every domestic slave is as much as before assured of his customary food and other allowances, and of a master's care in sickness and infirmity, even though the master class, and the country at large, have but half the previously existing profits, or value of capital. A striking proof of this was afforded by the recent (and still continuing) general suspension of payments of the banks in this country, and the consequent universal pecuniary loss and distress. Payments of debts could not be obtained, commodities could not be sold, and all manufacturing and some other great industrial operations either had to be continued for greatly reduced prices and wages, or to be entirely suspended, or if of such kind as could be suspended, in consequence, in the Northern States, the free hired laborers were thrown out of employment, or employed only at much reduced wages. Hence all such persons were greatly damaged or distressed, and thousands of the most destitute were ready to starve. Hence hunger mobs were menacing the city of New York with pillage, and the last evils of a vicious and unbridled and starving populace, excited to insurrection and defiance of legal authority. Universal loss from this cause also visited the slaveholding States, and every property holder, and also, to some extent, every other free man therein. But not a slave has lost a meal, or a comfort; and as a class, the slaves scarcely know of the occurrence of this great national calamity which has so universally damaged their masters, and the capitalists and employers of labor. Nor was the difference of effect owing to the slaves being generally engaged in agricultural labors. The very large business of manufacturing tobacco, in Virginia, is carried on almost exclusively by the labor of slaves, and those mostly hired by the year. The late bank suspension serving to suspend all payments of debts to, and income of, their great establishments, they were generally compelled to suspend work, even though still obliged to feed and support their hired slave laborers, who, for some time, thus received their full allowance and support, while remaining perfectly idle, and returning no compensation whatever to their employers who had hired them for the year.

THE "ASSOCIATED LABOR" DOCTRINE OF THE SOCIALISTS TRUE—
BUT DEFICIENT IN THE MAIN AGENCY, WHICH
SLAVERY ONLY CAN SUPPLY.

The socialists of Europe, and of the Northern States of this Union, (there are none existing in our Southern States,) of every sect, and however differing on other points, have all advocated the *association of labor*, in some form or other, as the great means for reforming the evils of society arising from starving competition for labor. The founders and preachers of socialism had all observed and earnestly appreciated these evils. They saw that, in advanced society, labor was the slave of capital, and that the more capital was enriched by the employment of labor, the less was acquired and retained by the individual laborers, and the more their wants and sufferings were increased. They also saw, and correctly, that there was great loss of time and labor in the domestic operations of every poor family, and most in the poorest families—and also, that the productive labors of all, if associated, and thus aiding each other, might be made much more productive. And if by laborers being associated in large numbers, and directed by their combined knowledge to the most profitable purposes and ends, all unnecessary waste (as occurs in isolated families) was prevented, and all the actual efforts of labor utilized—the net profits and economy of such associated labor would be much increased, and thus, the laborers might secure and retain a sufficient subsistence, out of the larger share of the profits of their labors, which now goes to the share of employers and capitalists. Their views and doctrines are true in the main, and are altogether so plausible, and so applicable to the wretched condition of labor in the most advanced conditions of society in Europe, that the teachers have found numerous believers and zealous disciples. Sundry associations have been originated in Europe, and established in America, (as a new country only offered the needed facilities), to carry out, in different modes, the great object of associating and combining labor, for the common and general profit and benefit. But every such attempt has met with signal, and also speedy, failure; except a few, of religious associations, which were under the guidance and direction of a single despotic head. In all other cases, no matter how benevolent and intelligent the leaders—and though one hour of labor, in each day, in this cheap and fertile country, would yield more food than fifteen hours' labor in Europe—still these associations soon failed in their every aim and purpose, and were severally broken up as soon as their inherent defects were made manifest, and seen to be inevitable and incurable incidents of the system.

Yet, so far as their facts and reasoning go, and in their main doctrines, the socialists are right. Associated labor can be much more productive, and be conducted more economically, than the labors of individual persons or families. The socialist theorists reasoned correctly, and in their practical experiments they devised good but defective plans. They constructed admirable and complex machinery to produce certain final results, in which every wheel and other operating agent was well adjusted as a secondary cause, or effect of another preceding cause. But in all these great and complicated works, the artificers had omitted to supply the first and great motive power, which is to be found only in one directing mind, and one controlling will. Supply the one supreme head and governing power to the association of labor, (for the suitable conditions of society,) and the scheme and its operation will become as perfect as can be expected of any human institution. But in supplying this single ruling power, the association is thereby converted to the condition of *domestic slavery*. And our system of domestic slavery offers in use, and to the greatest profit for all parties in the association, the realization of all that is sound and valuable in the socialists' theories and doctrines, and supplies the great and fatal defect of all their plans for practically associating labor. A few illustrative views will be submitted, which will apply to both the theoretical free associated labor, and to the practical domestic slave labor.

Suppose that some extensive industrial operation, as the tillage of a great farm, the working of a mine, or a cotton factory, is carried on by the labor of fifty men, with that of such other few members of their families as can be spared from home. These men, as usual, generally, are married, and have one or more young children. But whether single and without children, or husbands, or widowers with children, every man is the head of an isolated family, for which separate services are indispensable. Each home or family requires, and has, its separate purchasing of food, (and at retail and highest prices,) its separate cooking, washing, fires, lights, nursing of children, and of the sick, &c., &c. Such duties, in an ordinary or average family, fully occupy the time of the wife and mother. If there is no wife, or the mother is dead, the single man, or the father, is more or less required to perform the like household and woman's duties. Thus, of the supposed fifty households, probably including not less than from 150 to 200 persons, there may be but the fifty men to labor for wages. All the many others capable of labor, are fully employed as menial servants, and nurses for their respective families. This is necessarily the condition of free laborers, each working for himself and his family.

Now suppose, instead of this free population, that all the laborers and their families were slaves to the employer. Then, with proper and convenient arrangement of buildings, &c., instead of there being fifty women cooking, washing, and nursing the sick or the helpless of so many different small households, four or five might even better (with the better means and facilities afforded by the master) perform these services for all. This would dispense with some forty-five women, or other hands fit for labor, previously engaged in these household duties, and which would nearly double the number previously working for production and profit. This great increase of numbers would fully compensate for the general lessening of each individual's labor, which is certain of domestic slaves compared to free laborers driven by hunger. This abatement of toil, together with the allowances indispensable to the profitable existence of slavery, would render certain the comfortable subsistence of the slaves, which, if it could have been for free laborers, would ultimately have given way to the sufferings from competition and slavery, to want, and next to the pauper slavery now so general in England. Further, in this form of associated labor, there would be secured many of the savings in expenses which the socialists correctly counted upon, besides those already mentioned. By the single head and master providing all the necessaries for the maintenance and comfort of the laboring class, the contracts and purchases would be few and on a large scale, and at wholesale prices. There would not, at any time, be a deficiency of food, nor any necessary deficiency of medical or nursing attendance on the sick. When required by economy, fire and light could be supplied to all at half the cost that would be required separately for each family. Thus, in the institution of domestic slavery, and in that only, are most completely realized the dreams and sanguine hopes of the socialist school of philanthropists. Yet the socialists are all arrayed among the most fanatical and intolerant denouncers of domestic slavery, and the most malignant enemies of slaveholders. . . .

THORNTON STRINGFELLOW

A SCRIPTURAL VIEW OF SLAVERY.

THE SCRIPTURAL RECORD served the needs of Southern writers in a double
capacity. Purely historical justification for chattel servitude abounded in
Hebrew law and custom as well as in the institutions of the Roman Empire.
It seemed to follow that behind these historical sanctions, recognized as they
were in Holy Writ, also stood the higher sanctions of divine favor. The Old
Testament contained accounts of dealings in slaves by the patriarchs of
Israel, and in the New Testament—at a time when slavery was practiced
throughout the Roman world—the Apostles urged obedience to all secular
ordinances, including those governing the relations of master and servant.

One of the most forceful exponents of Scripture in defense of slavery was
the Reverend Thornton Stringfellow, a Baptist minister of Culpeper County,
Virginia. Stringfellow's widely read pamphlet essay, "A Scriptural View"—
substantial portions of which are reprinted here—covers the ground with
great thoroughness.

. . . I PROPOSE . . . TO EXAMINE the sacred volume briefly, and
if I am not greatly mistaken, I shall be able to make it appear that
the institution of slavery has received, in the first place,

1st. The sanction of the Almighty in the Patriarchal age.

2d. That it was incorporated into the only National Constitution
which ever emanated from God.

3d. That its legality was recognized, and its relative duties regulated, by Jesus Christ in his kingdom. . . .

The first recorded language which was ever uttered in relation to
slavery, is the inspired language of Noah. In God's stead he says,
"Cursed be Canaan;" "a servant of servants shall he be to his
brethren." "Blessed be the Lord God of Shem; and Canaan shall be

Scriptural and Statistical Views in Favor of Slavery (Richmond: J. W. Randolph, 1856), 4th ed., pp. 6-54, *passim;* also published as "The Bible Argument:
Or, Slavery in the Light of Divine Revelation," in E. N. Elliott, ed., *Cotton is
King; and Pro-Slavery Arguments* (Augusta: Pritchard, Abbott & Loomis,
1860), pp. 462-490, *passim.*

his servant." "God shall enlarge Japheth, and he shall dwell in the tents of Shem; and Canaan shall be his servant."—Gen. ix: 25, 26, 27. Here, language is used, showing the *favor* which God would exercise to the posterity of Shem. and Japheth, while they were holding the posterity of Ham in a state of *abject bondage.* May it not be said in truth, that God decreed this institution before it existed; and has he not connected its *existence* with prophetic tokens of special favor, to those who should be slave owners or masters? . . . The sacred records occupy but a short space from this inspired ray on this subject, until they bring to our notice, a man that is held up as a model, in all that adorns human nature, and as one that God delighted to honor. This man is Abraham, honored in the sacred records, with the appellation, "Father" of the "faithful." Abraham was a native of Ur, of the Chaldees. From thence the Lord called him to go to a country which he would show him; and he obeyed, not knowing whither he went. He stopped for a time at Haran, where his father died. From thence he "took Sarai his wife, and Lot his brother's son, and all their substance that they had gathered, and the souls they had gotten in Haran, and they went forth to go into the land of Canaan."—Gen. xii: 5.

All the ancient Jewish writers of note, and Christian commentators agree, that by the "souls they had gotten in Haran," as our translators render it, are meant their slaves, or those persons they had bought with their money in Haran. In a few years after their arrival in Canaan, Lot with all he had was taken captive. So soon as Abraham heard it, he armed three hundred and eighteen slaves that were born in his house, and retook him. How great must have been the entire slave family, to produce at this period of Abraham's life, such a number of young slaves able to bear arms.—Gen. xiv: 14. . . .

God had promised Abraham's seed the land of Canaan, and that in his seed all the nations of the earth should be blessed. He reached the age of eighty-five, and his wife the age of seventy-five, while as yet, they had no child. At this period, Sarah's anxiety for the promised seed, in connection with her age, induced her to propose a female slave of the Egyptian stock, as a secondary wife, from which to obtain the promised seed. This alliance soon puffed the slave with pride, and she became insolent to her mistress—the mistress complained to Abraham, the master. Abraham ordered Sarah to exercise her authority. Sarah did so, and pushed it to severity, and the slave absconded. The divine oracles inform us, that the angel of God found this run-away bond-woman in the wilderness; and if God had commissioned his angel to improve this opportunity of teaching the world how much he abhorred slavery, he took a bad plan to acomplish it. For, instead of repeating a homily upon doing to others as we "would they should do unto us," and heaping reproach upon Sarah, as a hypocrite, and Abraham as a tyrant, and giving Hagar direction how she might get into Egypt, from whence (according to abolitionism) she had been unrighteously sold into bondage, the angel addressed her as "Hagar, Sarah's maid,"—Gen. xvi: 1, 9; (thereby recognizing the relation of master and slave,) and asks her, "whither wilt thou go?" and she said "I flee from the face of my mistress." . . .

. . . Judge for yourself, reader, by the angel's answer: "And the angel of the Lord said unto her, Return unto thy mistress, and submit thyself under her hands."—Gen. xvi: 9.

But, says the spirit of abolition, with which the Bible has to contend, you are building your house upon the sand, for these were nothing but hired servants; and their servitude designates no such state, condition, or relation, as that, in which one person is made the property of another, to be bought, sold, or transferred forever. To this, we have two answers in reference to the subject, *before giving the law.* In the first place, the term servant, in the schedules of property among the patriarchs, *does designate* the state, condition, or relation in which one person is the legal property of another, as in Gen. xxiv: 35, 36. Here Abraham's servant, who had been sent by his master to get a wife for his son Isaac, in order to prevail with the woman and her family, states, that the man for whom he sought a bride, was the son of a man whom God had greatly blessed with riches; which he goes on to enumerate thus, in the 35th verse: "He hath given him flocks, and herds, and silver, and gold, and menservants, and maid-servants, and camels, and asses;" then in verse 36th, he states the disposition his master had made of his estate: "My master's wife bare a son to my master when she was old, and

unto him he hath given all that he hath." Here, servants are
enumerated with silver and gold as part of the patrimony. And,
reader, bear it in mind; as if to rebuke the doctrine of abolition,
servants are not only inventoried as property, but as property which
God had given to Abraham. After the death of Abraham, we have
a view of Isaac at Gerar, when he had come into the possession of
this estate; and this is the description given of him: "And the man
waxed great, and went forward, and grew until he became very
great; for he had possession of flocks, and possession of herds, and
great store of servants."—Gen. xxvi: 13, 14. This state in which
servants are made chattels, he received as an inheritance from his
father, and passed to his son Jacob.

Again, in Genesis xvii, we are informed of a covenant God entered
into with Abraham; in which he stipulates to be a God to him and
his *seed*, (not his servants,) and to give to his *seed* the land of
Canaan for an everlasting possession. He expressly stipulates, that
Abraham shall put the token of this covenant upon every servant
born in his house, and upon every servant *bought with his money
of any stranger*.—Gen. xvii: 12, 13. Here again servants are property. Again, more than four hundred years afterward, we find the
seed of Abraham, on leaving Egypt, directed to celebrate the rite,
that was ordained as a memorial of their deliverance, viz: the Pass-
over, at which time the same institution which makes *property of
men* and *women*, is recognized, and the *servant bought with money*,
is given the privilege of partaking, upon the ground of his being
circumcised *by his master*, while the hired servant, over whom the
master had no such control, is excluded until he *voluntarily* sub-
mits to circumcision; showing clearly that the institution of involuntary slavery then carried with it a right, on the part of the
master, *to choose* a religion *for the servant* who was his money, as
Abraham did, by God's direction, when he imposed circumcision
on those he had bought with his money,—when he was circumcised
himself, with Ishmael his son, who was the only individual beside himself, on whom he had a right to impose it, except the bond-
servants bought of the stranger with his money, and their children
born in his house. The next notice we have of servants as property,
is from God himself, when clothed with all the visible tokens of

his presence and glory, on the top of Sinai, when he proclaimed his law to the millions that surrounded its base: "Thou shalt not covet thy neighbor's house, thou shalt not covet thy neighbor's wife, nor his man-servant, nor his maid-servant, nor his ox, nor his ass, nor any thing that is thy neighbor's."—Ex. xx: 17. Here is a patriarchal catalogue of property, having God for its author, the wife among the rest, who was then purchased, as Jacob purchased his two, by fourteen years' service. Here the term servant, as used by the Almighty, under the circumstances of the case could not be understood by these millions, as meaning any thing but property, because the night they left Egypt, a few weeks before, Moses, by Divine authority, recognized their servants as property, which they had bought with their money. . . .

. . . Job himself was a great slaveholder, and, like Abraham, Isaac, and Jacob, won no small portion of his claims to character with God and men from the manner in which he discharged his duty to his slaves. Once more: the conduct of Joseph in Egypt, *as Pharaoh's counsellor*, under all the circumstances, proves him a friend to absolute šlavery, as a form of government better adapted to the state of the world at that time, than the one which existed in Egypt; for certain it is, that he peaceably effected a change in the fundamental law, by which a *state, condition, or relation,* between Pharaoh and the Egyptians was established, which answers to the one now denounced as sinful in the sight of God. Being warned of God, he gathered up all the surplus grain in the years of plenty, and sold it out in the years of famine, until he gathered up all the money; and when money failed, the `Egyptians came and said, "Give us bread;" and Joseph said, "Give your cattle, and I will give for your cattle, if money fail." When that year was ended, they came unto him the second year, and said, "There is not aught left in sight of my Lord, but our bodies and our lands. Buy us and our lands for bread." And Joseph bought all the land of Egypt for Pharaoh.

So the land became Pharaoh's, and as for the people, he removed them to cities, from one end of the borders of Egypt, even to the other end thereof. Then Joseph said unto the people, "Behold! I have bought you this day, and your land for Pharaoh; and they said, "we will be Pharaoh's servants."—See Gen. xlvii: 14, 16, 19, 20, 21, 23, 25. Having thus changed the fundamental law, and created a state of entire *dependence* and *hereditary bondage*, he enacted in his sovereign pleasure, that they should give Pharaoh one part, and take the other four parts of the productions of the earth to themselves. How far the hand of God was in this overthrow of liberty, I will not decide; but from the fact that he has singled out the greatest slaveholders of that age, as the objects of his special favor, it would seem that the institution was one furnishing great opportunities to exercise grace and glorify God, as it still does, where its duties are faithfully discharged.

. . . We will therefore proceed to our second proposition, which is—

Second.—That it was incorporated in the only national constitution emanating from the Almighty. By common consent, that portion of time stretching from Noah, until the law was given to Abraham's posterity, at Mount Sinai, is called the patriarchal age; *this is the period we have reviewed,* in relation to this subject. From the giving of the law until the coming of Christ, is called the Mosaic or legal dispensation. From the coming of Christ to the end of time, is called the Gospel dispensation. The legal dispensation *is the period of time, we propose now to examine,* in reference to the institution of involuntary and hereditary slavery; in order to ascertain, whether, during this period, *it existed at all,* and *if it did exist,* whether with the *divine sanction,* or in *violation of the divine will.* This dispensation is called the legal dispensation, because it was the pleasure of God to take Abraham's posterity by miraculous power, then numbering near three millions of souls, and give them a written constitution of government, a country to dwell in, and a covenant of special protection and favor, for their obedience to his law until the coming of Christ. The laws which he gave them emanated from his sovereign pleasure, and were designed, in the first place, to make himself known in his essential perfections; second, in his moral character; third, in his relation to man; and fourth, to make known those principles of action by the exercise of which man attains his highest moral elevation, viz: supreme love to God, and love to others as to ourselves.

. All the law is nothing but a preceptive exemplification of these two principles; consequently, the existence of a precept in the law, utterly irreconcilable with these principles, would destroy all claims upon us for an acknowledgment of its divine original. Jesus Christ himself has put his finger upon these two principles of human conduct, (Deut. vi: 5—Levit. xix: 18,) revealed in the law of Moses, and decided, that on them hang all the law and the prophets. . . .

. . . For the fifteen hundred years, during which these laws were in force, God raised up a succession of prophets to reprove that people for the various sins into which they fell; yet there is not a reproof uttered against the institution of *involuntary slavery*, for any species of abuse that ever grew out of it. A severe judgment is pronounced by Jeremiah, (chapter xxxiv: see from the 8th to the 22d verse,) for an abuse or violation of the law, concerning the *voluntary* servitude of Hebrews; but the prophet pens it with caution, as if to show that it had no reference to any abuse that had taken place under the system of *involuntary slavery*, which existed by law among that people; the sin consisted in making hereditary bond-men and bond-women of Hebrews, which was positively forbidden by the law, and not for buying and holding one of another nation in hereditary bondage, which was as positively allowed by the law. And really, in view of what is passing in our country, and elsewhere, among men who profess to reverence the Bible, it would seem that these must be dreams of a distempered brain, and not the solemn truths of that sacred book.

Well, I will now proceed to make them good to the letter, see Levit. xxv: 44, 45, 46; "Thy bond-men and thy bond-maids which thou shalt have, shall be of the heathen that are round about you; of them shall ye buy bond-men and bond-maids. Moreover, of the children of the strangers that do sojourn among you, of them shall ye buy, and of their families that are with you, which they begat in your land. And they shall be your possession. And ye shall take them as an inheritance for your children after you, to inherit them for a possession they shall be your bond-men forever." I ask any candid man, if the words of this institution could be more explicit? It is from God himself; it authorizes that people, to whom he had become *king and law-giver*, to purchase men and women as property; to hold them and their posterity in bondage; and to will them to their children as a possession forever; and more, it allows *foreign slaveholders* to *settle* and *live among them;* to *breed slaves* and *sell them.* Now, it is important to a correct understanding of this subject, to connect with the right to *buy* and *possess,* as property, the amount of authority *to govern,* which is granted by the *lawgiver;* this amount of authority is implied, in the first place, in the law which prohibits the exercise of rigid authority upon the Hebrews, who are allowed to sell themselves for limited times. "If thy brother be waxen poor, and be sold unto thee, thou shalt not *compel him* to serve as a *bond servant,* but as a *hired servant,* and as a *sojourner* he shall be with thee, and shall serve thee until the year of jubilee—*they shall not be sold as bond-men;* thou *shalt not rule over them with rigor."*—Levit. xxv: 39, 40, 41, 42, 43. It will be evident to all, that here are *two states* of servitude; in reference to *one* of which, *rigid* or *compulsory* authority, is *prohibited,* and that its *exercise is authorized in the other.*

Second.—In the criminal code, that conduct is punished with death, when done to a *freeman,* which is not punishable at all, when done *by a master to a slave,* for the express reason, that the slave is the *master's money.* "He that smiteth a man so that he die, shall surely be put to death."—Exod. xxi: 20, 21. "If a man smite his servant or his maid, with a rod, and he die under his hand, he shall be surely punished; notwithstanding, if he continue a day or two, he shall not be punished, for he is his money."—Exod. xxi: 20. Here is precisely the same crime: smiting a man so that he die; if it be a freeman, he shall surely be put to death, whether the man die under his hand, or live a day or two after; but if it be a servant, and the master continued the rod until the servant died under his hand, then it must be evident that such a chastisement could not be necessary for any purpose of wholesome or reasonable authority, and therefore he may be punished, but not with death. But if the death did not take place for a day or two, then it is to be *presumed,* that the master only aimed to use the rod, so far as was necessary to produce subordination, and for this, the law which allowed him to lay out his money in the slave, would protect him against all punishment. This is the common-sense principle which has been adopted substantially in civilized countries, where involuntary slavery has been instituted, from that day until this. . . .

Again, the divine Law-giver, in guarding the property right in slaves among his chosen people, sanctions principles which may work the separation of man and wife, father and children. . . . "If thou buy a Hebrew servant, six years shall he serve thee, and in the seventh he shall go out free for nothing; if he came in by himself, he shall go out by himself; if he were married, then his wife shall go out with him; if his master have given him a wife (one of his bond-maids) and she have borne him sons and daughters, the wife and her children shall be her master's and he shall go out by himself."—Exod. xxi: 2, 3, 4. Now, the God of Israel gives this man the option of being separated by the master, from his wife and children, or becoming himself a servant forever, with a mark of the fact, like our cattle, in the ear, that can be seen wherever he goes; for it is enacted, "If the servant shall plainly say, I love my master, my wife, and my children, I will not go out free, then his master shall bring him unto the judges, (in open court,) he shall also bring him unto the door, or unto the door post, (so that all in the court-house, and those in the yard may be witnesses, and his master shall bore his ear through with an awl; and he shall serve him forever." It is useless to spend more time in gathering up what is written in the Scriptures on this subject, from the giving of the law until the coming of Christ. . . . We propose—

Third. To show that Jesus Christ recognized this institution as one that was lawful among men, and regulated its relative duties.

. . . I affirm then, first, (and no man denies,) that Jesus Christ has not abolished slavery by a prohibitory command: and second, I affirm, he has introduced no new moral principle which can work its destruction, under the gospel dispensation; and that the principle relied on for this purpose, is a fundamental principle of the Mosaic law, under which slavery was instituted by Jehovah himself: and third, with this absence of positive prohibition, and this absence of principle, to work its ruin, I affirm, that in all the Roman provinces, where churches were planted by the apostles, hereditary slavery existed, as it did among the Jews, and as it does now among us, (which admits of proof from history that no man will dispute who knows any thing of the matter,) and that in instructing such churches, the Holy Ghost by the apostles, has recognized the institution, as one *legally existing* among them, to be perpetuated in the church, and that its duties are prescribed.

Now for the proof: To the church planted at Ephesus, the capital of the lesser Asia, Paul ordains by letter, subordination in the fear of God,—first between wife and husband; second, child and parent; third, servant and master; *all, as states, or conditions, existing among the members.*

The relative duties of each state are pointed out; those between the servant and master in these words: "Servants be obedient to them who are your masters, according to the flesh, with fear and trembling, in singleness of your heart as unto Christ; not with eye service as men pleasers, but as the servants of Christ, doing the will of God from the heart, with good-will, doing service, as to the Lord, and not to men, knowing that whatsoever good thing any man doeth, the same shall he receive of the Lord, whether he be bond or free. And ye masters do the same things to them, forbearing threatening, knowing that your master is also in heaven, neither is there respect of persons with him." Here, by the Roman law, the servant was property, and the control of the master unlimited, as we shall presently prove.

To the church at Colosse, a city of Phrygia, in the lesser Asia, —Paul in his letter to them, recognizes the three relations of wives and husbands, parents and children, servants and masters, as relations existing among the members; (here the Roman law was the same;) and to the servants and masters he thus writes: "Servants obey in all things your masters, according to the flesh: not with eye service, as men pleasers, but in singleness of heart, fearing God: and whatsoever you do, do it heartily, as to the Lord and not unto men; knowing that of the Lord ye shall receive the reward of the inheritance, for ye serve the Lord Christ. But he that doeth wrong shall receive for the wrong he has done; and there is no respect of persons with God. Masters give unto your servants that which is just and equal, knowing that you also have a master in heaven."

The same Apostle writes a letter to the church at Corinth;— a very important city, formerly called the eye of Greece, either from its location, or intelligence, or both, and consequently, an important point, for radiating light in all directions, in reference to subjects connected with the cause of Jesus Christ; and particularly, in the bearing of its practical precepts on civil society, and the political structure of nations. Under the direction of the Holy Ghost, he instructs the church, that, on this particular subject, *one general principle* was ordained of God, applicable alike in all countries and at all stages of the church's future history, and that it was this: "*as the Lord has called every one, so let him walk.*" "Let every man abide in the same calling wherein he is called." "Let every man wherein he is called, therein abide with God."—1 Cor. vii: 17, 20, 24. "*And so ordain I in all churches;*" vii: 17. The Apostle thus explains his meaning:

"Is any man called being circumcised? Let him not become un-circumcised."

"Is any man called in uncircumcision? Let him not be circumcised."

"Art thou called, being a servant? Care not for it, but if thou mayest be made free, use it rather;" vii: 18, 21. Here, by the Roman law, slaves were property,—yet Paul ordains, in this, and all other churches, that Christianity gave them no title to freedom, but on the contrary, required them not to care for being slaves, or in other words, to be contented with their *state*, or *relation*, unless they could be *made free*, in a lawful way.

Again, we have a letter by Peter, who is the Apostle of the circumcision—addressed especially to the Jews, who were scattered through various provinces of the Roman empire; comprising those provinces especially, which were the theater of their dispersion, under the Assyrians and Babylonians. . . . He thus instructs them: "Submit yourselves to every ordinance of man for the Lord's sake." "For so is the will of God." "Servants, be subject to your masters with all fear, not only to the good and gentle, but also to the froward."—1 Peter ii: 11, 13, 15, 18. What an important document is this! enjoining political subjection to *governments of every form,* and Christian subjection on the part of servants to their masters, whether good or bad; for the purpose of showing forth to advantage, the *glory of the gospel,* and putting to silence the ignorance of foolish men, who might think it seditious.

By "every ordinance of man," as the context will show, is meant governmental regulations or laws, as was that of the Romans for enslaving their prisoners taken in war, instead of destroying their lives.

When such enslaved persons came into the church of Christ let them (says Peter) "be subject to their masters with all fear," whether such masters be good or bad. It is worthy of remark, that he says much to secure civil subordination to the State, and hearty and cheerful obedience to the masters, on the part of servants; yet he says nothing to masters in the whole letter. It would seem from this, that danger to the cause of Christ was on the side of *insubordination among the servants,* and a *want of humility with inferiors,* rather than *haughtiness among superiors* in the church. . . .

. . . It is taken for granted, on all hands pretty generally, that Jesus Christ has at least been silent, or that he has not personally spoken on the subject of slavery. Once for all, I deny it. Paul, after stating that a slave was to honor an unbelieving master, in the 1st verse of the 6th chapter, says, in the 2d verse, that to a believing master, he is the rather to do service, because he who partakes of the benefit is his brother. He then says, if any man teach otherwise, (as all abolitionists then did, and now do,) and consent not to wholesome words, "even the words of our Lord Jesus Christ." Now, if our Lord Jesus Christ uttered such words, how dare we say he has been silent? If he has been silent, how dare the Apostle say these are the words of our Lord Jesus Christ, if the Lord Jesus Christ never spoke them? . . .

We will remark, in closing under this head, that we have shown from the text of the sacred volume, that when God entered into covenant with Abraham, it was with him as a slaveholder; that when he took his posterity by the hand in Egypt, five hundred years afterward to confirm the promise made to Abraham, it was

done with them as slaveholders; that when he gave them a constitution of government, he gave them the right to perpetuate
hereditary slavery; and that he did not for the fifteen hundred years
of their national existence, express disapprobation toward the institution.

We have also shown from authentic history that the institution
of slavery existed in every family, and in every province of the
Roman Empire, at the time the gospel was published to them.

We have also shown from the New Testament, that all the
churches are recognized as composed of masters and servants;
and that they are instructed by Christ how to discharge their relative duties; and finally that in reference to the question which
was then started, whether Christianity did not abolish the institution, or the right of one Christian to hold another Christian in
bondage, we have shown, that "the words of our Lord Jesus Christ"
are, that so far from this being the case, it adds to the obligation
of the servant to render service with good-will to his master, and
that gospel fellowship is not to be entertained with persons who
will not consent to it! . . .

GEORGE FREDERICK HOLMES
(1820-1897)

REVIEW OF UNCLE TOM'S CABIN.

BORN IN BRITISH GUIANA, George Frederick Holmes came to Virginia at the age of eighteen. There he taught school, studied law, turned to writing, married the governor's daughter, and eventually settled down as a college professor. After temporary sojourns at William and Mary and the University of Mississippi, interspersed with tours of free-lancing, he was appointed in 1857 to the University of Virginia's chair of History and Literature, which he occupied with distinction for the remaining forty years of his life.

The literary vehicle that suited Holmes best was the lengthy review essay —a form in which no Southern writer excelled him—and it was through his many reviews in *DeBow's*, the *Southern Literary Messenger*, and the *Southern Quarterly Review* during the 1850s that Holmes exerted his greatest influence. His ideas on slavery as a "sociologically" indispensable arrangement were similar to those of Henry Hughes and George Fitzhugh. Indeed, Fitzhugh wrote him early in 1855, after reading Holmes's enthusiastic article on *Sociology for the South*: "You and Hughes and I in the last year, it seems to me, have revolutionized public opinion in the South on the subject of slavery."

In 1852 the *Southern Literary Messenger*, gasping for breath, was not expected to live out the year. But the *Messenger's* editor, John R. Thompson, was determined not to let his magazine expire before it had assaulted Harriet Beecher Stowe with "as strong a review of 'Uncle Tom's Cabin' as it is within the wit of man to contrive," and Thompson thought the obvious man for the work was George Frederick Holmes. In a vein of brooding intensity he wrote Holmes: "I would have the review as hot as hell fire, blasting and searing the reputation of the vile wretch in petticoats who could write such a volume. . . . I want it *to tell* throughout the length and breadth of the land, so that whenever Uncle Tom's Cabin is mentioned, by an inevitable association, men shall call up the Messenger's annihilation of its author." Holmes obliged with ten thousand hot and indignant words.

A portion of the review is reprinted here.

"Uncle Tom's Cabin," *Southern Literary Messenger*, XVIII (December 1852), pp. 721-731.

THIS IS A FICTION—professedly a fiction; but, unlike other works of the same type, its purpose is not amusement, but proselytism. The romance was formerly employed to divert the leisure, recreate the fancy, and quicken the sympathies of successive generations, changing its complexion and enlarging the compass of its aims with the expanding tastes of different periods; but never forgetting that its main object was to kindle and purify the imagination, while fanning into a livelier flame the slumbering charities of the human heart. But, in these late and evil days, the novel, notwithstanding those earlier associations, has descended from its graceful and airy home, and assumed to itself a more vulgar mission, incompatible with its essence and alien to its original design. Engaging in the coarse conflicts of life, and mingling in the fumes and gross odours of political or polemical dissension, it has attained and tainted the robe of ideal purity with which it was of old adorned. . . .

We have examined the production of Mrs. Harriet Beecher Stowe, which we purpose to review, and we discover it to belong to the latter class, and to be one of the most reprehensible specimens of the tribe. We own that we approach the criticism of the work with peculiar sensations of both reluctance and repugnance. We take no pleasure in the contact with either folly or vice; and we are unwilling to handle the scandalous libel in the manner in which it deserves to be treated, in consideration of its being the effusion of one of that sex, whose natural position entitles them to all forbearance and courtesy, and which, in all ordinary cases, should be shielded even from just severity, by that protecting mantle which the name and thought of woman cast over even the erring and offending members of the sex. But higher interests are involved; the rule that everyone bearing the name and appearance of a lady, should receive the delicate gallantry and considerate tenderness which are due to a lady, is not absolutely without exception. If she deliberately steps beyond the hallowed precincts—the enchanted circle—which encompasses her as with the halo of divinity, she has wantonly forfeited her privilege of immunity as she has irretrievably lost our regard, and the harshness which she may provoke is invited by her own folly and impropriety. We cannot accord to the termagant virago or the foul-mouthed hag the same deference that is rightfully due to the maiden purity of untainted innocence. Still, though the exception undoubtedly exists, and we might, without indecorum, consider that all claims to forbearance had been lost by Mrs. Stowe, we shall not avail ourselves of the full benefit of her forfeiture. We cannot take the critical lash into our hands with the same callous indifference, or with the same stern determination of venting our just indignation, that we might have done, had the penalty been required for 'the lords of creation.' We will endeavor, then, as far as possible, to forget Mrs. Harriet Beecher Stowe, and the individuality of her authorship, and will strive to concentrate our attention and our reprehension on her book. . . .

We have said that Uncle Tom's Cabin is a fiction. It is a fiction throughout; a fiction in form; a fiction in its facts; a fiction in its representations and coloring; a fiction in its statements; a fiction in its sentiments; a fiction in its morals; a fiction in its religion; a fiction in its inferences; a fiction equally with regard to the subjects it is designed to expound, and with respect to the manner of their exposition. It is a fiction, not for the sake of more effectually communicating truth; but for the purpose of more effectually disseminating a slander. It is a fictitious or fanciful representation for the sake of producing fictitious or false impressions. Fiction is its form and falsehood is its end. . . .

In Uncle Tom's Cabin, the vice of this depraved application of fiction and its desolating consequences, may be readily detected. Every fact is distorted, every incident discolored, in order to awaken rancorous hatred and malignant jealousies between the citizens of the same republic, the fellow countrymen whose interests and happiness are linked with the perpetuity of a common union, and with the prosperity of a common government. With the hope of expediting or achieving the attainment of a fanatical, and in great measure, merely speculative idea, of substituting the real thraldom of free labor for the imaginary hardships of slavery—the hydra of dissension is evoked by the diabolical spells of falsehood, misrepresentation, and conscious sophistry. What censure shall we pass upon a book, calculated, if not designed, to produce such a result? What condemnation upon an effort to revive all the evils of civil discord—to resuscitate all the dangers of disunion—allayed

with such difficulty, and but recently lulled into partial quiescence
by the efforts of the sages and the patriotic forbearance of the
States of the Confederacy? What language shall we employ when
such a scheme is presented, as the *beau ideal* of sublimated virtue,
under the deceptive form of literary amusement, and is seriously
offered as the recreation of our intellectual leisure?

. . . We will concede for the nonce, the general truth of the facts
alleged, and will maintain that, notwithstanding this concession,
the culpability of the work, its fallacy and its falsehood remain
the same. In the one case, the false conclusions are erected upon
the basis of false assertions; in the other, we overlook the untruth
of the statements, and find that they are deliberately employed
for the insinuation of untrue and calumnious impressions. We will
suppose, then, that such enormities as are recounted in Uncle Tom's
Cabin, do occur at the South: that George Harris and Eliza his
wife, with that seraphic little mulatto, their child, have, in truth,
their prototypes among our slaves, and that the brutal treatment
of the former by his owner, might find its parallel in actual life.
We will endeavor to imagine the reality of the murder of Prue,
and the probability of the virtues, misfortunes and martyrdom of
Uncle Tom—and, still heavier tax upon our credulity, we will suppose the angelical mission of that shrewish Yankee maiden, Miss
Ophelia, for the conversion of hopeless niggers, and the redemption
of Ebo, to have been a fact:—and, yet, notwithstanding all this,
and it is tough, indeed, to swallow, we will maintain the doctrines
of the book to be most pernicious, the representation given to be
the most erroneous, the impression designed to be produced the
most criminal and false, and the iniquity of the scandalous production to be entitled to unmitigated censure and reprobation. We
will not even limit our concession so far as might be requisite to
bring the delineation within any reasonable approximation of the
truth; we will not insist that the incidents conceded must be regarded as exceptional cases; for it is perceived in Uncle Tom's
Cabin, that to admit them to be exceptions, would be to change,
entirely, the character of the argument, and destroy its validity.
How acute is the perverse instinct of deliberate wrong: how sagacious the ingenuity of premeditated error? we will concede all

the facts stated in the work: all that we will not concede, is the significance attributed to them, and their relevancy for the purpose for which they are employed. And, having granted all this, we still believe that we can offer an ample vindication of the South, and justify the severest censure of this inflammatory and seditious production.

We cannot, however, pass to what may be regarded as the argument of the work, without noting that the hero and heroine of the tale—the tawny Apollo and Venus, with the interesting yellow Cupid, on whom so large a portion of the plot is concentrated—belong exactly to that particular shade of tainted blood, when the laws of many of the Southern States, if not of all, would recognize them as free. George and Eliza Harris, as represented, have a larger proportion of white blood in their veins, than is compatible with the continuance of the servile condition. . . .

But leaving this exceedingly vulnerable characteristic of Uncle Tom's Cabin, the argument of the work—for there is an argument even in successive dramatic pictures designed to produce a given effect, as well as in successive syllogisms designed to establish a special conclusion:—the argument of the work is, in plain and precise terms, that any organization of society—any social institution, which can by possibility result in such instances of individual misery, or generate such examples of individual cruelty as are exhibited in this fiction, must be criminal in itself, a violation of all the laws of Nature and of God, and ought to be universally condemned, and consequently immediately abolished. Unhappily, in all the replies to Uncle Tom's Cabin which have hitherto been attempted under the form of corresponding fiction, usually, we are sorry to say, by weak and incompetent persons, it has not been recognized with sufficient distinctness that the whole strength of the attack, as the whole gist of the argument, lies in this thesis. The formal rejoinders have consequently been directed to the wrong point: the real question has been mistaken; and the formal issue never joined. This explains the insufficiency of such counter representations as Aunt Phillis's Cabin, and similar apologies; and also that sense of insufficiency which they have not failed to produce. It is no valid refutation of the offensive fiction that slavery may be shown to present at times—no matter how frequently—a very different phase. This point was already guarded:—nay, it was already conceded in Uncle Tom's Cabin; and such a mode of replication consequently mistakes the subject of debate, and is entirely without force because directed against a post already surrendered. It may be doubted, indeed, whether an assault on a solemn interest, moral or social, conveyed under the garb of fiction, can ever be satisfactorily answered under a similar form. If it could be, it would be too trivial to be worthy of such an elaborate defence. If it be sufficiently important to demand a thorough reply, it is degrading to the serious character of the subject, it is trifling with the earnest and grave import of the question, to dress it up in the gewgaws and tawdry finery of a mere counter-irritant. Moreover, a reply in this shape too commonly necessitates such an adherence to the dramatic procedure and to the progression of sentiment adopted by the original work, that it places the replicant in a secondary position, and exhibits him in the false light of a mere imitator and plagiarist, by way of opposition, thus obviously yielding the vantage ground to the offender. If, however, the reply must be couched in the same form as the attack, the true picture to be delineated is not a mere representation of a real or imaginary state of beatitude enjoyed by fictitious slaves, but should be the portraiture of graver miseries, worse afflictions, and more horrible crimes familiar to the denizens of our Northern cities, and incident to the condition of those societies where the much lauded white labor prevails. But the main cause of failure in the replies which have been attempted, and whose inefficacy has been injurious to the interests of the South, has unquestionably been that the real thesis of Uncle Tom's Cabin, whence most of its dangers, its pernicious sophistry, and its wicked delusion proceed, has not been recognized with adequate clearness, and has not been refuted in a suitable manner. It is this thesis which we propose to examine.

The true and sufficient reply to this proposition is a very brief one. It is simply this, that the position is absolutely fatal to all human society—to all social organization, civilized or savage, whatever. It strikes at the very essence and existence of all community among men, it lays bare and roots up all the foundations of law, order and government. It is the very evangel of insubordination, sedition, and anarchy, and is promulgated in support of a cause worthy of the total ruin which it is calculated to produce. Pandemonium itself would be a paradise compared with what all society would become, if this apparently simple and plausible position were tenable, and action were accordingly regulated by it. Ate herself, hot from hell, could not produce more mischievous or incurable disorder than this little thesis, on which the whole insinuated argument of Uncle Tom's Cabin is founded, if this dogma were once generally or cordially received. In all periods of history—under all forms of government—under all the shifting phases of the social condition of man, instances of misery and barbarity equal to any depicted in this atrocious fiction, have been of constant recurrence, and, whatever changes may hereafter take place, unless the nature of man be also changed, they must continually recur until the very end of time. In thousands of instances, of almost daily occurrence, the affliction or the crime has sprung as directly from existing laws, manner, and institutions, as in the examples erroneously charged to the score of slavery in Uncle Tom's Cabin. But in all of them the real causes have been the innate frailties of humanity, the play of fortuitous circumstances, the native wickedness of particular individuals, and the inability of human wisdom or legislation to repress crime without incidentally ministering to occasional vices. If there be any latent truth in the dogma enforced by the nefarious calumnies of Uncle Tom's Cabin, it furnishes a stronger argument against all other departments of social organization than it does against slavery, as the records of our courts of justice and the inmates of our penitentiaries would testify. There is no felon who might not divest himself of his load of guilt, and extricate his neck from the halter, if such an argument was entitled to one moment's weight or consideration. . . .

It is no distinctive feature of the servile condition that individual members of the class should suffer most poignantly in consequence of the crimes, the sins, the follies, or the thoughtlessness of others;—that children should be torn from their parents, husbands separated from their wives, and fathers rudely snatched away from their families. The same results, with concomitant infamy, are daily produced by the operation of all penal laws, and the same anguish and distress are thereby inflicted upon the helpless and innocent, yet such laws remain and must remain upon our statute books for the security and conservation of any social organization at all. The ordinary play of human interests, of human duties, of human necessities, and even of human ambition—unnoticed and commonplace as it may be conceived to be, produce scenes more terrible and agony more poignant and heart-rending than any attributed to slavery in Uncle Tom's Cabin. The temptations of wordly advancement, the hopes of temporary success, the lures of pecuniary gain, in every civilized or barbarous community throughout the world—in the deserts of Sahara as amid the snows of Greenland—in the streets of Boston and Lowell as in those of London, Manchester, and Paris, may and do exhibit a longer register of sadder results than even a treacherous imagination, or fiction on the hunt for falsehood has been able to rake up from the fraudulent annals of slavery in the present work. There is scarcely one revolution of a wheel in a Northern or European cotton-mill, which does not, in its immediate or remote effects, entail more misery on the poor and the suffering than all the incidents of servile misery gathered in the present work from the most suspicious and disreputable sources. The annual balance sheet of a Northern millionaire symbolizes infinitely greater agony and distress in the labouring or destitute classes than even the foul martyrdom of Uncle Tom. Are the laws of debtor and creditor—and the processes by which gain is squeezed from the life-blood of the indigent, more gentle;—or the hard, grasping, demoniac avarice of a yankee trader more merciful than the atrocious heart of that fiendish yankee, Simon Legrèe? Was the famine in Ireland productive of no calamities which might furnish a parallel to the scenes in Uncle Tom's Cabin? We would hazard even the assertion that the Australian emigration from Great Britain, and the California migration in our country—both impelled by the mere hope of sudden and extraordinary gains, have been attended with crimes and vices, sorrows, calamities and distresses far surpassing the imaginary ills of the slaves whose fictitious woes are so hypocritically bemoaned. But such are the incidents of life, and we would

neither denounce nor revolutionize society, because such consequences were inseparable from its continuance.

It should be observed that the whole tenor of this pathetic tale
derives most of its significance and colouring from a distorted representation or a false conception of the sentiments and feelings of
the slave. It presupposes an identity of sensibilities between the
races of the free and the negroes, whose cause it pretends to advocate. It takes advantage of this presumption, so suspiciously
credited where slavery is unknown, to arouse sympathies for what
might be grievous misery to the white man, but is none to the
differently tempered black. Every man adapts himself and his feelings more or less to the circumstances of his condition: without
this wise provision of nature life would be intolerable to most of
us. Every race in like manner becomes habituated to the peculiar
accidents of its particular class; even the Paria may be happy.
Thus what would be insupportable to one race, or one order of
society, constitutes no portion of the wretchedness of another. The
joys and the sorrows of the slave are in harmony with his position,
and are entirely dissimilar from what would make the happiness,
or misery, of another class. It is therefore an entire fallacy, or
a criminal perversion of truth, according to the motive of the
writer, to attempt to test all situations by the same inflexible rules,
and to bring to the judgment of the justice of slavery the prejudices
and opinions which have been formed when all the characteristics
of slavery are not known but imagined.

The proposition, then, which may be regarded as embodying the
peculiar essence of Uncle Tom's Cabin, is a palpable fallacy, and
inconsistent with all social organization. Granting, therefore, all
that could be asked by our adversaries, it fails to furnish any proof
whatever of either the iniquity or the enormity of slavery. If it
was capable of proving anything at all, it would prove too much.
It would demonstrate that all order, law, government, society was a
flagrant and unjustifiable violation of the rights, and mockery of
the feelings of man and ought to be abated as a public nuisance.
The hand of Ishmael would thus be raised against every man, and
every man's hand against him. To this result, indeed, both the
doctrines and practices of the higher-law agitators at the North,

and as set forth in this portentous book of sin, unquestionably
tend: and such a conclusion might naturally be anticipated from
their sanctimonious professions. The fundamental position, then, of
these dangerous and dirty little volumes is a deadly blow to all
the interests and duties of humanity, and is utterly impotent to
show any inherent vice in the institution of slavery which does
not also appertain to all other institutions whatever. But we will
not be content to rest here: we will go a good bow-shot beyond this
refutation, though under no necessity to do so; and we maintain
that the distinguishing characteristic of slavery is its tendency to
produce effects exactly opposite to those laid to its charge; to diminish the amount of individual misery in the servile classes; to
mitigate and alleviate all the ordinary sorrows of life; to protect
the slaves against want as well as against material and mental
suffering; to prevent the separation and dispersion of families; and
to shield them from the frauds, the crimes, and the casualties of
others, whether masters or fellow-slaves, in a more eminent degree
than is attainable under any other organization of society, where
slavery does not prevail. This is but a small portion of the peculiar
advantages to the slaves themselves resulting from the institution
of slavery, but these suffice for the present, and furnish a most over-
whelming refutation of the philanthropic twaddle of this and similar
publications.

Notwithstanding the furious and ill-omened outcry which has
been made in recent years against the continuance of slavery, the
communities where it prevails exhibit the only existing instance of
a modern civilized society in which the interests of the labourer
and the employer of labour are absolutely identical, and in which
the reciprocal sympathies of both are assured. The consequence
is that both interest and inclination, the desire of profit and the
sense or sentiment of duty concur to render the slave-owner considerate and kind toward the slave. So general is the feeling, so
habitual the consciousness of this intimate harmony of the interests
and duties of both, that it has formed an efficient public sentiment
at the South which brands with utter reprobation the slaveholder
who is either negligent of his slaves or harsh in his treatment of
them. It goes even further than this; it makes every man at the

South the protector of the slave against injury by whomsoever offered, thus establishing an efficient and voluntary police, of which
every one is a member, for the defence of the slave against either
force, fraud, or outrage. Such habitual regard for the rights of a
subordinate class generates in its members a kindliness of feeling
and a deference of bearing to the slaveholder in general, which no
severity could produce and no rigor maintain. It is this intercom-
munion of good offices and good will, of interests and obligations,
which renders the realities of slavery at the South so entirely different from what they are imagined to be by those who have no
intimate familiarity with its operation. Hence, too, in great measure
it is, that, except where inveterate idleness or vice compels a sale,
or the changes of fortune, or the casualties of life, break up an
establishment, families are rarely dispersed, but are held together
without being liable to those never-ending separations which are
of daily occurrence with the labouring or other classes elsewhere.
Even where the misfortunes of the owner necessitate a sale, if the
negroes enjoy a respectable character, there is every possibility
that they will never be removed from the district in which they
have lived, but will either be bought with the place on which they
have worked, be transferred *en masse* to some neighboring locality,
or scattered about within easy distance of each other in the same
vicinity.

It is true that the continued agitation of the slavery question,
and the nefarious practices of the abolitionists, which are so
cordially eulogised in Uncle Tom's Cabin, have in some degree
modified the relations between master and slave in those frontier
settlements which border on the Ohio river, and have rendered imperative a harsher intercourse and more rigid management, than
prevails where the feelings and principles of the negroes are not
tampered with by incendiary missionaries. This is but one of the
melancholy fruits of that philanthropical fanaticism, which injures
by every movement which it makes those whom it pretends so
sympathetically to serve.

It is needless to repeat the evidence that the average condition
of the slave at the South is infinitely superior, morally and materially, in all respects, to that of the labouring class under any

other circumstances in any other part of the world. This has been done so frequently and efficiently before, that we need only refer to previous expositions of this point. . . .

We are surprised to see how small a portion of the topics of censure, to which the production is obnoxious, has yet been touched upon: to feel that after all we have already said, the mountain of its offences, its perversions, its fallacies, and its iniquities, still rises as vast as ever before us. We have not had the heart to speak of an erring woman as she deserved, though her misconduct admitted of no excuse, and provoked the keenest and most just reprobation. We have little inclination—and, if we had much, we have not the time, to proceed with our disgusting labor: to anatomize minutely volumes as full of poisonous vermin as of putrescence, and to speak in such language as the occasion would justify, though it might be forbidden by decorum and self-respect.

We dismiss Uncle Tom's Cabin with the conviction and declaration that every holier purpose of our nature is misguided, every charitable sympathy betrayed, every loftier sentiment polluted, every moral purpose wrenched to wrong, and every patriotic feeling outraged, by its criminal prostitution of the high functions of the imagination to the pernicious intrigues of sectional animosity, and to the petty calumnies of willful slander.

DAVID CHRISTY (1802-1867)

COTTON IS KING.

THE POSITION OF DAVID CHRISTY among the pro-slavery writers would have to be regarded as somewhat ambiguous if it were simply a question of personal commitment, since he was not a Southerner and not an out-and-out defender of slavery. But the popularity of Christy's *Cotton is King* was not in the least ambiguous; the book was enthusiastically accepted in the South as a powerful contribution to the pro-slavery argument. Christy, one of the two Northerners represented in the present collection, was a journalist of Cincinnati (the gateway of the Ohio River trade with the South) and a one-time agent of the American Colonization Society in Ohio, where the Society's principal concern was ridding the state of free Negroes. Although Christy seems not to have approved wholly of slavery, he was far more concerned by what he thought was the foolish futility of the abolitionist crusade. The result was *Cotton is King*, which turned out to be the most brilliantly "realistic" of all the arguments in support of Negro slavery. The impersonal power of "King Cotton" had created a vast web of interdependent relationships involving production, labor, manufacturing, and markets which bound the North, the South, and Europe together in an indivisible system-of-mutual prosperity. It was inevitable that "King Cotton," whose rule was both beneficent and despotic, should stifle any and all efforts to disrupt the perfection of his empire.

Christy's book was first published in 1855 and went through three editions. There were passages in it which referred to slavery as an "evil," but the intensity of the author's moral feelings must be judged by the use to which he allowed his book to be put. He sold the copyright in 1860 to E. N. Elliott so that the latter might include the work in a large compendium of pro-slavery thought which he was bringing out that year, with express permission for the editor to make any textual changes he wished. Few were actually made besides the erasing of references to "evil" which smudged the original in one or two places.

The excerpt printed below is taken from Christy's first edition of 1855, and includes selections from the Introduction, Chapter II, and Conclusion.

Cotton is King: Or the Culture of Cotton, and Its Relation to Agriculture, Manufactures and Commerce; to the Free Colored People; and to Those who Hold that Slavery is in itself Sinful (Cincinnati: Moore, Wilstach, Keys & Co., 1855), pp. 10-11, 36-45, 184-192; reprinted in E. N. Elliott, ed., *Cotton Is King, and Pro-Slavery Arguments* (Augusta: Pritchard, Abbott & Loomis, 1860), pp. 33-34, 55-60, 215-226.

THE CONTROVERSY ON SLAVERY in the United States, has been one of an exciting and complicated character. The power to *emancipate* existing, in fact, in the States separately, and not in the General Government, the efforts to abolish it, by appeals to public opinion, have been fruitless, except when confined to single States. In Great Britain, the question was simple. The power to abolish Slavery in her West Indian colonies was vested in Parliament. To agitate the people of England, and call out a full expression of sentiment, was to control Parliament, and secure its abolition. The success of the English Abolitionists, in the employment of moral force, had a powerful influence in modifying the policy of American Anti-slavery men. Failing to discern the difference in the condition of the two countries, they attempted to create a public sentiment throughout the United States, adverse to Slavery, in the confident expectation of speedily overthrowing the institution. The issue taken, that Slavery is *malum in se*—a sin in itself—was prosecuted with all the zeal and eloquence they could command. Churches, adopting the *per se* doctrine, inquired of their converts, not whether they supported Slavery, by the use of its products, but whether they believed the institution itself sinful. Could public sentiment be brought to assume the proper ground; could the Slaveholder be convinced that the world denounced him as equally criminal with the robber and murderer; then, it was believed, he would abandon the system. Political parties, subsequently organized, taught, that to vote for a Slaveholder, or a Pro-slavery man, was sinful, and could not be done without violence to conscience; while, at the same time, they made no scruples of using the products of Slave labor—the exorbitant demand for which was the great bulwark of the institution. This was a radical error. It laid all who adopted it open to the charge of practical inconsistency, and left them without any moral power over the consciences of others. As long as all used their products, so long the Slaveholders found the *per se* doctrine working them no harm; as long as no provision was made for supplying the demand for tropical products, by free labor, so long there was no risk in extending the field of their operations. Thus, the very things necessary to the overthrow of American Slavery, were left undone, while those essential to its prosperity, were continued in the most active operation; so that, now, after nearly a "thirty years' war," we may say, emphatically, COTTON IS KING, and his enemies are vanquished. . . .

The institution of Slavery, at this moment, gives indications of a vitality that was never anticipated by its friends or foes. Its enemies often supposed it about ready to expire, from the wounds they had inflicted, when in truth it had taken two steps in advance; while they had taken twice the number in an opposite direction. In each successive conflict, its assailants have been weakened, while its dominion has been extended.

This has arisen from causes too generally overlooked. Slavery is not an isolated system, but is so mingled with the business of the world, that it derives facilities from the most innocent transactions. Capital and labor, in Europe and America, are largely employed in the manufacture of cotton. These goods, to a great extent, may be seen freighting every vessel, from Christian nations, that traverses the seas of the globe; and filling the warehouses and shelves of the merchants, over two-thirds of the world. By the industry, skill, and enterprise, employed in the manufacture of cotton, mankind are better clothed; their comfort better promoted; general industry more highly stimulated; commerce more widely extended; and civilization more rapidly advanced, than in any preceding age.

To the superficial observer, all the agencies, based upon the manufacture and sale of cotton, seem to be legitimately engaged in promoting human happiness; and he, doubtless, feels like invoking Heaven's choicest blessings upon them. When he sees the stockholders in the cotton corporations receiving their dividends, the operatives their wages, the merchants their profits, and civilized people everywhere clothed comfortably in cottons, he can not refrain from explaining: "The lines have fallen unto them in pleasant places; yea, they have a goodly heritage!"

But turn a moment to the source whence the raw cotton, the basis of these operations, is obtained, and observe the aspect of things in that direction. When the statistics on the subject are examined, it appears that nearly all the cotton consumed in the Christian world, is the product of the Slave labor of the United

States. It is this monopoly that has given Slavery its commercial value; and, while this monopoly is retained, the institution will continue to extend itself wherever it can find room to spread. He who looks for any other result, must expect that nations, which, for centuries, have waged war to extend their commerce, will now abandon their means of aggrandizement, and bankrupt themselves, to force the abolition of American Slavery!

This is not all. The economical value of Slavery as an agency for supplying the means of extending manufactures and commerce, has long been understood by statesmen. The discovery of the power of steam, and the inventions in machinery, for preparing and manufacturing cotton, revealed the important fact, that a single Island, having the monopoly secured to itself, could supply the world with clothing. *Great Britain attempted to gain this monopoly;* and, to prevent other countries from rivaling her, she long prohibited all emigration of skillful mechanics from the kingdom, as well as all exports of machinery. As country after country was opened to her commerce, the markets for her manufactures were extended, and the demand for the raw material increased. The benefits of this enlarged commerce of the world, were not confined to a single nation, but mutually enjoyed by all. As each had products to sell, peculiar to itself, the advantages often gained by one, were no detriment to the others. The principal articles demanded by this increasing commerce, have been coffee, sugar, and cotton—in the production of which Slave labor has greatly predominated. Since the enlargement of manufactures, cotton has entered more extensively into commerce than coffee and sugar, though the demand for all three has advanced with the greatest rapidity. England could only become a great commercial nation, through the agency of her manufactures. She was the best supplied, of all the nations, with the necessary capital, skill, labor, and fuel, to extend her commerce by this means. But, for the raw material, to supply her manufactories, she was dependent upon other countries. The planters of the United States were the most favorably situated for the cultivation of cotton, and attempted *to monopolize the markets for that staple.* This led to a fusion of interests between them and the manufacturers of Great Britain; and to the invention of notions, in political economy, that would, so far as adopted, promote the interests of this coalition. With the advantages possessed by the English manufacturers, "Free Trade" would render all other nations subservient to their interests; and, so far as their operations should be increased, just so far would the demand for American cotton be extended. The details of the success of the parties to this combination, and the opposition they have had to encounter, are left to be noticed more fully hereafter. To the cotton planters, the copartnership has been eminently advantageous.

How far the other agricultural interests of the United States are promoted, by extending the cultivation of cotton, may be inferred from the Census returns of 1850, and the Congressional Reports on Commerce and Navigation, for 1854. Cotton and tobacco, only, are largely exported. The production of sugar does not yet equal our consumption of the article, and we import, chiefly from Slave-labor countries, 445,445,680 lbs. to make up the deficiency. But of cotton and tobacco, we export more than *two-thirds* of the amount produced; while of other products, of the agriculturists, less than the *one-forty-sixth* part is exported. Foreign nations, generally, can grow their provisions, but can not grow their tobacco and cotton. Our surplus provisions, not exported, go to the villages, towns, and cities, to feed the mechanics, manufacturers, merchants, professional men, and others; or to the cotton and sugar districts of the South, to feed the planters and their slaves. The increase of mechanics and manufacturers at the North, and the expansion of Slavery at the South, therefore, augment the markets for provisions, and promote the prosperity of the farmer. As the mechanical population increases, the implements of husbandry, and articles of furniture, are multiplied, so that both farmer and planter can be supplied with them on easier terms. As foreign nations open their markets to cotton fabrics, increased demands, for the raw material, are made. As new grazing and grain-growing States are developed, and teem with their surplus productions, the mechanic is benefited, and the planter, relieved from food-raising, can employ his slaves more extensively upon cotton. It is thus that our exports are increased; our foreign commerce advanced; the home markets of the mechanic and farmer extended, and the wealth of the nation promoted. It is thus, also, that the Free labor of the country finds remunerating markets for its products— though at the expense of serving as an efficient auxiliary in the extension of Slavery!

But more. So speedily are new grain-growing States springing up; so vast is the territory owned by the United States, ready for settlement; and so enormous will soon be the amount of products demanding profitable markets, that the national government has been seeking new outlets for them, upon our own continent, to which, alone, they can be advantageously transported. That such outlets, when our vast possessions, Westward, are brought under cultivation, will be an imperious necessity, is known to every statesman. The farmers of these new States, after the example of those of the older sections of the country, will demand a market for their products. This can be furnished, only, by the extension of Slavery; by the acquisition of more tropical territory; by open-ing the ports of Brazil, and other South American countries, to the admission of our provisions; or by a vast enlargement of domestic manufactures, to the exclusion of foreign goods from the country. Look at this question as it now stands, and then judge of what it must be twenty years hence. The class of products under consideration, in the whole country, in 1853, were valued at $1,551,-176,490; of which there were exported to foreign countries, to the value of only $33,809,126. The planter will not assent to any check upon the foreign imports of the country, for the benefit of the farmer. This demands the adoption of vigorous measures to secure a market for his products by some of the other modes stated. Hence, the orders of our Executive, in 1851, for the exploration of the valley of the Amazon; the efforts, in 1854, to obtain a treaty with Brazil for the free navigation of that immense river; the negotiations for a military foothold in St. Domingo, and the determination to acquire Cuba. . . .

CONCLUSION.

In concluding our labors, there is little need of extended observa-tion. The work of Emancipation, in our country, was checked, and the extension of Slavery promoted:—first, by the Free Colored

People neglecting to improve the advantages afforded them; second, by the increasing values imparted to Slave-labor; third, by the mistaken policy into which the Abolitionists have fallen. Whatever reasons might now be offered, for emancipation, from an improvement of our Free colored people, is far more than counterbalanced by its failure in the West Indies, and the constantly increasing value of the labor of the Slave. If, when the Planters had only a moiety of the markets for Cotton, the value of Slavery was such as to arrest emancipation, how must the obstacles be increased, now, when they have the monopoly of the markets of the world?

We propose not to speak of remedies for Slavery. That we leave to others. Thus far this great civil and social evil, has baffled all human wisdom. Either some radical defect must have existed, in the measures devised for its removal, or the time has not yet come for successfully assailing the Institution. Our work is completed, in the delineation we have given of its varied relations to our commercial and social interests. As the monopoly of the culture of Cotton, imparts to Slavery its economical value, the system will continue as long as this monopoly is maintained. Slave-Labor products have now become necessities of human life, to the extent of more than half the commercial articles supplied to the Christian world. Even Free labor, itself, is made largely subservient to Slavery, and vitally interested in its perpetuation and extension.

Can this condition of things be changed? It may be reasonably doubted, whether anything efficient can be speedily accomplished: not because there is lack of territory where freemen may be employed in tropical cultivation; not because intelligent free-labor is less productive than slave-labor; but because freemen, whose constitutions are adapted to tropical climates, will not avail themselves of the opportunity offered for commencing such an enterprise.

KING COTTON cares not whether he employs slaves or freemen. It is the *cotton*, not the *slaves*, upon which his throne is based. Let freemen do his work as well, and he will not object to the change. Thus far the experiments in this respect have failed, and they will not soon be renewed. The efforts of his most powerful ally, Great Britain, to promote that object, have already cost her people many hundreds of millions of dollars: with total failure as a reward for her zeal. One-sixth of the colored people of the United States are free; *but they shun the cotton regions,* and have been instructed to detest *emigration to Liberia.* Their improvement has not been such as was anticipated; and their more rapid advancement cannot be expected, while they remain in the country. The free colored people of the West Indies, can no longer be relied on to furnish tropical products, for they are fast sinking into savage indolence. His MAJESTY, KING COTTON, therefore, is forced to continue the employment of his slaves; and, by their toil, is riding on, conquering and to conquer! He receives no check from the cries of the oppressed, while the citizens of the world are dragging forward his chariot, and shouting aloud his praise!

KING COTTON is a profound statesman, and knows what measures will best sustain his throne. He is an acute mental philosopher, acquainted with the secret springs of human action, and accurately perceives who will best promote his aims. He has no evidence that colored men can grow his cotton, but in the capacity of slaves. It is his policy, therefore, to defeat all schemes of emancipation. To do this, he stirs up such agitations as lure his enemies into measures that will do him no injury. The venal politician is always at his call, and assumes the form of saint or sinner, as the service may demand. Nor does he overlook the enthusiast, engaged in Quixotic endeavors for the relief of suffering humanity, but influences him to advocate measures which tend to tighten, instead of loosing the bands of Slavery. Or, if he cannot be seduced into the support of such schemes, he is beguiled into efforts that waste his strength on objects the most impracticable—so that Slavery receives no damage from the exuberance of his philanthropy. But should such a one, perceiving the futility of his labors, and the evils of his course, make an attempt to avert the consequences; while he is doing this, some new recruit, pushed forward into his former place, charges him with lukewarmness, or Pro-slavery sentiments, destroys his influence with the public, keeps alive the delusions, and sustains the supremacy of KING COTTON in the world.

In speaking of the economical connections of Slavery with the other material interests of the world, we have called it a *tri-partite alliance.* It is more than this. It is *quadruple.* Its structure includes

our parties, arranged thus: The Western Agriculturists; the South-
rn Planters; the English Manufacturers; and the American Aboli-
ionists! By this arrangement, the Abolitionists do not stand in
lirect contact with Slavery:—they imagine, therefore, that they
lave clean hands and pure hearts, so far as sustaining the system
s concerned. But they, no less than their allies, aid in promoting the
nterests of Slavery. Their sympathies are with England on the
Ilavery question, and they very naturally incline to agree with her
in other points. She advocates *Free Trade*, as essential to her manu-
actures and commerce; and they do the same, not waiting to in-
[uire into its bearings upon *American Slavery*. We refer now to the
Ieople, not to their leaders, whose integrity we choose not to indorse.
[he Free Trade and Protective Systems, in their bearings upon
Ilavery, are so well understood, that no man of general reading,
:specially an editor, who professes Anti-Slavery sentiments, at the
ame time advocating Free Trade, will ever convince men of intel-
igence, pretend what he may, that he is not either woefully
Ierverted in his judgment, or emphatically, a "dough-face" in dis-
[uise! England, we were about to say, is in alliance with the cotton
Ilanter, to whose prosperity Free Trade is indispensable. Abolition-
sm is in alliance with England. All three of these parties, then,
Igree in their support of the Free Trade policy. It needed but the
Iid of the Western Farmer, therefore, to give permanency to this
Irinciple. His adhesion has been given, the *quadruple alliance* has
Ieen perfected, and Slavery and Free Trade *nationalized!*

The crisis now upon the country, as a consequence of Slavery
Iaving become dominant, demands that the highest wisdom should
Ie brought to the management of national affairs. The *quacks* who
Iave aided in producing the malady, and who have the effrontery
:till to claim the right to manage the case, must be dismissed. The
nen who mock at the Political Economy of the North, and have
Issisted in crushing its cherished policy, must be rebuked. Slavery,
Iationalized, can now be managed only as a national concern. It can
Iow be abolished only with the consent of those who sustain it.
[heir assent can be gained only on employing other agents to meet
Ihe wants it now supplies. It must be superseded, then, if at all, by
neans that will not injuriously affect the interests of commerce and

agriculture, to which it is now so important an auxiliary. To supply the demand for tropical products, except by the present mode, is not the work of a day, nor of a generation. Should the influx of foreigners continue, such a change may be possible. But to effect the transition from Slavery to Freedom, on principles that will be acceptable to the parties who control the question; to devise and successfully sustain such measures as will produce this result; must be left to statesmen of broader views and loftier conceptions than are to be found among those at present engaged in this great controversy. . . .

JAMES HENRY HAMMOND (1807-1864)

"MUD-SILL" SPEECH.

BEGINNING HIS CAREER AS a lawyer and editor in South Carolina, James H. Hammond eventually acquired great wealth both through his marriage and from the successful management of several large plantations. He was twice elected governor and served in both houses of Congress. He delighted in authorship, wrote extensively in support of slavery, and enjoyed the friendship of the South's leading men of letters. The following is a selection from a speech he made in the Senate in reply to one by William H. Seward on the proposed admission of Kansas in 1858. Several elements of the standard pro-slavery argument may be discerned in it: the "King Cotton" theory, the class struggle inherent in Northern "wage slavery," and the Aristotelian notion of superior and subordinate social functions. On this last point, the coarse metaphor—"mud-sill"—which Hammond used gained for the speech considerable notoriety.

. . . . No, YOU DARE NOT make war on cotton. No power on earth dares to make war upon it. Cotton *is* king. Until lately the Bank of England was king; but she tried to put her screws as usual, the fall before the last, upon the cotton crop, and was utterly vanquished. The last power has been conquered. Who can doubt, that has looked at recent events, that cotton is supreme? When the abuse of credit had destroyed credit and annihilated confidence; when thousands of the strongest commercial houses in the world were coming down, and hundreds of millions of dollars of supposed property evaporating in thin air; when you came to a dead lock, and revolutions were threatened, what brought you up? Fortunately for you it was the commencement of the cotton season, and we have poured in

"Speech on the Admission of Kansas," U. S. Senate, March 4, 1858, *Selections from the Letters and Speeches of the Hon. James H. Hammond, of South Carolina* (New York: John F. Trow & Co., 1866), pp. 317-322; *Congressional Globe*, 35 Cong., 1 Sess., pp. 961-962.

upon you one million six hundred thousand bales of cotton just at
the crisis to save you from destruction. That cotton, but for the
bursting of your speculative bubbles in the North, which produced
the whole of this convulsion, would have brought us $100,000,000.
We have sold it for $65,000,000, and saved you. Thirty-five million
dollars we, the slaveholders of the South, have put into the charity
box for your magnificient financiers, your "cotton lords," your
"merchant princes."

But, sir, the greatest strength of the South arises from the harmony of her political and social institutions. This harmony gives
her a frame of society, the best in the world, and an extent of
political freedom, combined with entire security, such as no other
people ever enjoyed upon the face of the earth. Society precedes
government; creates it, and ought to control it; but as far as we can
look back in historic times we find the case different; for government is no sooner created than it becomes too strong for society,
and shapes and moulds, as well as controls it. In later centuries the
progress of civilization and of intelligence has made the divergence
so great as to produce civil wars and revolutions; and it is nothing
now but the want of harmony between governments and societies
which occasions all the uneasiness and trouble and terror that we
see abroad. It was this that brought on the American Revolution.
We threw off a Government not adapted to our social system, and
made one for ourselves. The question is, how far have we succeeded?
The South, so far as that is concerned, is satisfied, harmonious, and
prosperous, but demands to be let alone.

In all social systems there must be a class to do the menial duties,
to perform the drudgery of life. That is, a class requiring but a low
order of intellect and but little skill. Its requisites are vigor, docility,
fidelity. Such a class you must have, or you would not have that
other class which leads progress, civilization, and refinement. It
constitutes the very mud-sill of society and of political government;
and you might as well attempt to build a house in the air, as to
build either the one or the other, except on this mud-sill. Fortunately for the South, she found a race adapted to that purpose to
her hand. A race inferior to her own, but eminently qualified in
temper, in vigor, in docility, in capacity to stand the climate, to

answer all her purposes. We use them for our purpose, and call them slaves. We found them slaves by the common "consent of mankind," which, according to Cicero, "*lex naturae est.*" The highest proof of what is Nature's law. We are old-fashioned at the South yet; slave is a word discarded now by "ears polite;" I will not characterize that class at the North by that term; but you have it; it is there; it is everywhere; it is eternal.

The Senator from New York said yesterday that the whole world had abolished slavery. Aye, the *name*, but not the *thing;* all the powers of the earth cannot abolish that. God only can do it when he repeals the *fiat*, "the poor ye always have with you;" for the man who lives by daily labor, and scarcely lives at that, and who has to put out his labor in the market, and take the best he can get for it; in short, your whole hireling class of manual laborers and "operatives," as you call them, are essentially slaves. The difference between us is, that our slaves are hired for life and well compensated; there is no starvation, no begging, no want of employment among our people, and not too much employment either. Yours are hired by the day, not cared for, and scantily compensated, which may be proved in the most painful manner, at any hour in any street in any of your large towns. Why, you meet more beggars in one day, in any single street of the city of New York, than you would meet in a lifetime in the whole South. We do not think that whites should be slaves either by law or necessity. Our slaves are black, of another and inferior race. The *status* in which we have placed them is an elevation. They are elevated from the condition in which God first created them, by being made our slaves. None of that race on the whole face of the globe can be compared with the slaves of the South. They are happy, content, unaspiring, and utterly incapable, from intellectual weakness, ever to give us any trouble by their aspirations. Yours are white, of your own race; you are brothers of one blood. They are your equals in natural endowment of intellect, and they feel galled by their degradation. Our slaves do not vote. We give them no political power. Yours do vote, and, being the majority, they are the depositaries of all your political power. If they knew the tremendous secret, that the ballot-box is stronger than "an army with banners," and could combine, where would you be? Your society would be reconstructed, your government over-thrown, your property divided, not as they have mistakenly at-tempted to initiate such proceedings by meeting in parks, with arms in their hands, but by the quiet process of the ballot-box. You have been making war upon us to our very hearthstones. How would you like for us to send lecturers and agitators North, to teach these people this, to aid in combining, and to lead them?

Mr. Wilson and others. Send them along.

Mr. Hammond. You say send them along. There is no need of that. Your people are awaking. They are coming here. They are thundering at our doors for homesteads, one hundred and sixty acres of land for nothing, and Southern Senators are supporting them. Nay, they are assembling, as I have said, with arms in their hands, and demanding work at $1,000 a year for six hours a day. Have you heard that the ghosts of Mendoza and Torquemada are stalking in the streets of your great cities? That the inquisition is at hand? There is afloat a fearful rumor that there have been consulta-tions for Vigilance Committees. You know what that means.

Transient and temporary causes have thus far been your pres-ervation. The great West has been open to your surplus popula-tion, and your hordes of semibarbarian immigrants, who are crowd-ing in year by year. They make a great movement, and you call it progress. Whither? It is progress; but it is progress towards Vigi-lance Committees. The South have sustained you in a great mea-sure. You are our factors. You fetch and carry for us. One hundred and fifty million dollars of our money passes annually through your hands. Much of it sticks; all of it assists to keep your ma-chinery together and in motion. Suppose we were to discharge you; suppose we were to take our business out of your hands;—we should consign you to anarchy and poverty. You complain of the rule of the South; that has been another cause that has preserved you. We have kept the Government conservative to the great purposes of the Con-stitution. We have placed it, and kept it, upon the Constitution; and that has been the cause of your peace and prosperity. The Senator from New York says that that is about to be at an end; that you intend to take the Government from us; that it will pass from our hands into yours. Perhaps what he says is true; it may be; but do not forget—it can never be forgotten—it is written on the brightest page of human history—that we, the slaveholders of the South, took our country in her infancy, and, after ruling her for sixty out of the seventy years of her existence, we surrendered her to you without a stain upon her honor, boundless in prosperity, incalculable in her strength, the wonder and the admiration of the world. Time will show what you will make of her; but no time can diminish our glory or your responsibility.

JOSIAH NOTT (1804-1873)

TYPES OF MANKIND.

THE JUSTIFICATION OF SLAVERY as an abstract principle might be—and was—drawn from history, Scripture, expediency, and the nature of human society. But the particular form, Negro slavery, which was practiced in this country needed also to be justified on grounds of race. That there was such a thing as "race," that the races differed in their capacities, and that the black race was inferior to the white, were assumptions held more or less pragmatically since colonial times. It remained only to give them the full warrant of scientific law.

It was here that the nearest thing to an intellectual schism in the pro-slavery ranks occurred. According to the Book of Genesis, mankind sprang from a single origin, the divergence and differentiation of the races having occurred in relatively recent times. Interpreted broadly, this could still leave room not only for exceptional members of any race but for the possibility of general improvement among them all. The latest findings of science, however, seemed to call the Biblical story of Creation into some question. Comparative studies of skulls, together with researches in Egyptian monuments, apparently showed that there were fundamental differences in structure and cranial capacity, and that such differences had been set in their present form thousands of years earlier than had previously been assumed. From this it was deduced that the races of mankind had not descended from a single source after all, but had had separate origins, and that they should actually be considered as separate species. The implications of this were resisted by many of the Southern clergy, but since the main orthodoxy, slavery, remained inviolate this little inconsistency could not have made much difference to Southern society at large.

Josiah Nott was a physician of Mobile who made a variety of contributions to medical technique and theory. He was also profoundly interested in ethnology, having long admired the work of Samuel Morton, and he made extensive studies of his own in that realm. His major preoccupation was the plural origin of races. This, plus the connection it had in Nott's mind with Negro slavery, may be seen in the selection that follows. It is

Types of Mankind: Or, Ethnological Researches Based upon the Ancient Monuments, Paintings, Sculptures, and Crania of Races, and Upon Their Natural, Geographical, Philological, and Biblical History . . . (Philadelphia: 1854), pp. 49-61.

the Introduction to a massive book, *Types of Mankind,* which was published by Nott and George R. Gliddon in 1854 and which eventually ran through ten editions.

MR. LUKE BURKE, the bold and able Editor of the *London Ethnological Journal,* defines Ethnology to be "a science which investigates the mental and physical differences of Mankind, and the organic laws upon which they depend; and which seeks to deduce from these investigations, principles of human guidance, in all the important relations of social existence." To the same author are we indebted not only for the most extensive and lucid definition of this term, but for the first truly philosophic view of a new and important science that we have met with in the English language.

The term "Ethnology" has generally been used as synonymous with "Ethnography," understood as the Natural History of Man; but by Burke it is made to take a far more comprehensive grasp— to include the whole mental and physical history of the various Types of Mankind, as well as their social relations and adaptations; and, under this comprehensive aspect, it therefore interests equally the philanthropist, the naturalist, and the statesman. Ethnology demands to know what was the primitive organic structure of each race?—what such race's moral and psychical character?—how far a race may have been, or may become, modified by the combined action of time and moral and physical causes?—and what position in the social scale Providence has assigned to each type of man?

"Ethnology divides itself into two principal departments, the *Scientific* and the *Historic.* Under the former is comprised every thing connected with the Natural History of Man and the fundamental laws of living organisms; under the latter, every fact in civil history which has any important bearing, directly or indirectly, upon the question of races—every fact calculated to throw light upon the number, the moral and physical peculiarities, the early seats, migrations, conquests or interblendings, of the primary divisions of the human family, or of the leading mixed races which have sprung from their intermarriages."

Such is the scope of this science—born, we may say, within our own generation—and we propose to examine mankind under the above two-fold aspect, while we point out some of the more salient results towards which modern investigation is tending. The press everywhere teems with new books on the various partitions of the wide field of Ethnology; yet there does not exist, in any language, an attempt, based on the highest scientific lights of the day, at a systematic treatise on Ethnology in its extended sense. MORTON was the first to conceive the proper plan; but, unfortunately, lived not to carry it out; and although the present volume falls very far below the just requirements of science, we feel assured that it will at least aid materially in suggesting the right direction to future investigators.

The grand problem, more particularly interesting to all readers, is that which involves the *common origin* of races; for upon the latter deduction hang not only certain religious dogmas, but the more practical question of the equality and perfectibility of races—we say "more practical question," because, while Almighty Power, on the one hand, is not responsible to Man for the distinct origin of human races, these, on the other, are accountable to Him for the manner in which their delegated power is used towards each other.

Whether an original diversity of races be admitted or not, the *permanence* of existing physical types will not be questioned by any Archaeologist or Naturalist of the present day. Nor, by such competent arbitrators, can the consequent permanence of moral and intellectual peculiarities of types be denied. The intellectual man is inseparable from the physical man; and the nature of the one cannot be altered without a corresponding change in the other.

The truth of these propositions had long been familiar to the master-mind of JOHN C. CALHOUN; who regarded them to be of such paramount importance as to demand the fullest consideration from those who, like our lamented statesman in his day, wield the destinies of nations and of races. An anecdote will illustrate the pains-taking laboriousness of Mr. Calhoun to let no occasion slip whence information was attainable. Our colleague, G. R. GLIDDON, happened to be in Washington City, early in May, 1844, on business of his father (United States' Consul for Egypt) at the State Department; at which time Mr. Calhoun, Secretary of State, was conducting diplomatic negotiations with France and England, connected with the annexation of Texas. Mr. Calhoun, suffering from indisposition, sent a message to Mr. Gliddon, requesting a visit at his lodgings. In a long interview which ensued, Mr. Calhoun stated, that England pertinaciously continued to interfere with our inherited Institution of Negro Slavery, and in a manner to render it imperative that he should indite very strong instructions on the subject to the late MR. WM. R. KING, of Alabama, then our Ambassador to France. He read to Mr. Gliddon portions of the manuscript of his celebrated letter to Mr. King, which, issued on the 12th of the following August, ranks among our ablest national documents. Mr. Calhoun declared that he could not foresee what course the negotiation might take, but wished to be forearmed for any emergency. He was convinced that the true difficulties of the subject could not be fully comprehended without first considering the radical difference of humanity's races, which he intended to discuss, should he be driven to the necessity. Knowing that Mr. Gliddon had paid attention to the subject of African ethnology; and that, from his long residence in Egypt, he had enjoyed unusual advantages for its investigation, Mr. Calhoun had summoned him for the purpose of ascertaining what were the best sources of information in this country. Mr. Gliddon, after laying before the Secretary what he conceived to be the true state of the case, referred him for further information to several scientific gentlemen, and more particularly to DR. MORTON, of Philadelphia. A correspondence ensued between Mr. Calhoun and Dr. Morton on the subject, and the Doctor presented to him copies of the *Crania Americana* and *Aegyptiaca*, together with minor works, all of which Mr. Calhoun studied with no less pleasure than profit. He soon perceived that the conclusions which he had long before drawn from history, and from his personal observations in America, on the Anglo-Saxon, Celtic, Teutonic, French, Spanish, Negro, and Indian races, were entirely corroborated by the plain teachings of modern science. He beheld demonstrated in Morton's works the important fact, that the Egyptian, Negro, several White, and sundry Yellow races, had existed, in their present forms, for at least 4000 years; and that it behoved the statesman to lay aside all current speculations about the origin and perfectibility of races, and to deal, in political argument, with the simple facts as they stand.

What, on the vital question of African Slavery in our Southern States, was the utilitarian consequence of Calhoun's memorable dispatch to King? Strange, yet true, to say, although the English press anxiously complained that Mr. Calhoun had intruded *Ethnology* into diplomatic correspondence, a communication from the Foreign Office promptly assured our Government that Great Britain had no intention of intermeddling with the domestic institutions of other nations. Nor, from that day to this, has she violated her formal pledge in our regard. During a sojourn of Mr. Calhoun, on his retirement from office, with us at Mobile, we enjoyed personal opportunities of knowing the accuracy of the above facts, no less than of receiving ample corroborations illustrative of the *inconvenience* which true ethnological science might have created in philanthropical diplomacy, had it been frankly introduced by a CALHOUN.

No class of men, perhaps, understand better the practical importance of Ethnology than the statesmen of England; yet from motives of policy, they keep its agitation studiously out of sight. DR. PRICHARD, when speaking of a belief in the diversity of races, justly remarks—

"If these opinions are not every day expressed in this country [England], it is because the avowal of them is restrained by a degree of odium that would be excited by it."

Although the press in that country has been, to a great extent, muzzled by government influence, we are happy to see that her periodicals are beginning to assume a bolder and more rational tone; and we may now hope that the stereotyped errors of Prichard, and we might add, those of Latham, will soon pass at their true value. The immense evils of false philanthropy are becoming too glaring to be longer overlooked. While, on the one hand, every true philanthropist must admit that no race has a right to enslave or oppress the weaker, it must be conceded, on the other, that all changes in existing institutions should be guided, not by fanaticism and groundless hypotheses, but by experience, sound judgment, and real charity. . . .

In the broad field and long duration of Negro life, not a single civilization, spontaneous or borrowed, has existed, to adorn its gloomy past. The ancient kingdom of Meroë has been often pointed out as an exception, but this is now proven to be the work of Pharaonic Egyptians, and not of Negro races. Of Mongolian races, we have the prolonged semi-civilizations of China, Japan, and (if they be classed under the same head) the still feebler attempts of Peru and Mexico. What a contrast, if we compare with these,

> "Caucasian progress, as exhibited in the splendid succession of distinct civilizations, from the ancient Egyptian to the recent Anglo-American, to which the Caucasian part of the species has given birth."

Nor when we examine their past history, their anatomical and physiological characters, and philological differences, are we justified in throwing all the Indo-European and Semitic races into one indivisible mass. . . .

Looking back over the world's history, it will be seen that human progress has arisen mainly from the war of races. All the great impulses which have been given to it from time to time have been the results of conquests and colonizations. Certain races would be stationary and barbarous for ever, were it not for the introduction of new blood and novel influences; and some of the lowest types are hopelessly beyond the reach even of these salutary stimulants to melioration. . . .

Dr. James Cowles Prichard, for the last half century, has been the grand orthodox authority with the advocates of a common origin for the races of men. His ponderous work on the "Physical History of Mankind" is one of the noblest monuments of learning and labour to be found in any language. It has been the never-exhausted reservoir of knowledge from which most subsequent writers on Ethnology have drawn; but, nevertheless, as Mr. Burke has sagely remarked, Prichard has been the "victim of a false theory." He commenced, when adolescent, by writing a graduating thesis, at Edinburgh, in support of the *unity of races,* and the remainder of his long life was devoted to the maintenance of this first impression. We behold him, year after year, like a bound giant, struggling with increasing strength against the cords which cramp him, and we are involuntarily looking with anxiety to see him burst them asunder. But how few possess the moral power to break through a deep-rooted prejudice! . . .

Albeit, in his last edition, Prichard evidently perceived, in the distance, a glimmer of light dawning from the time-worn monuments of "Old Egypt," destined eventually to dispel the obfuscations with which he had enshrouded the history of Man; and to destroy that darling unitary fabric on which all his energies had been expended. Had he lived but two years longer, until the mighty discoveries of LEPSIUS were unfolded to the world, he would have realized that the honorable occupation of his long life had been only to accumulate facts, which, properly interpreted, shatter everything he had built upon them. In the preface to vol. iii., he says:

"If it should be found that, within the period of time to which historical testimony extends, the distinguishing characters of human races have been constant and undeviating, it would become a matter of great difficulty to reconcile this conclusion [*i. e.* the unity of all mankind,] with the inferences already obtained from other considerations."

In other words, if hypotheses, and deductions drawn from analogies among the lower animals, should be refuted by well-ascertained facts, demonstrative of the absolute independence of the primitive types of mankind of all existing moral and physical causes, during several thousand years, Prichard himself concedes, that every argument heretofore adduced in support of a common origin for human families must be abandoned.

One of the main objects of this volume is to show, that the criterion-point, indicated by Prichard, is now actually arrived at; and that the diversity of races must be accepted by Science as a *fact*, independently of theology, and of all analogies or reasonings drawn from the animal kingdom.

It will be observed that, with the exception of Morton's, we seldom quote works on the Natural History of Man; and simply for the reason, that their arguments are all based, more or less, on fabled analogies, which are at last proved by the monuments of Egypt and Assyria to be worthless. The whole method of treating the subject is herein changed. To our point of view, most that has been written on human Natural History becomes obsolete; and therefore we have not burthened our pages with citations from authors, even the most erudite and respected, whose views we consider the present work to have, in the main, superseded.

Such is not our course, however, where others have anticipated any conclusion we may have attained; and we are happy to find that Jacquinot had previously recognized the principle which has overthrown Prichard's unitary scheme:

"If the great branches of the human family have remained distinct in the lapse of ages, with their characteristics fixed and unalterable, we are justified in regarding mankind as divisible into *distinct species.*"

Four years ago, in our "Biblical and Physical History of Man," we published the following remarks:—

"If the *Unity* of the Races or Species of Men be assumed, there are but three suppositions on which the *diversity* now seen in the white, black, and intermediate colors, can be accounted for, viz.:

"1st. A *miracle*, or direct act of the Almighty, in changing one type into another.

"2d. The gradual action of Physical causes, such as climate, food, mode of life, &c.

"3d. Congenital, or accidental varieties.

"There being no evidence whatever in favor of the first hypothesis, we pass it by. The second and third have been sustained with signal ability by Dr. Prichard, in his Physical History of Mankind."

Although, even then, thoroughly convinced ourselves that the second and third hypotheses were already refuted by facts, and that they would soon be generally abandoned by men of science, we confess that we had little hope of seeing this triumph achieved so speedily; still less did we expect, in this matter-of-fact age, to behold a *miracle*, which exists too, not in the Bible, but only in feverish imaginations, assumed as a scientific solution. Certain sectarians of the evangelical school are now gravely attempting, from lack of argument, to revive the old hypothesis of a miraculous change of one race into many at the Tower of Babel! Such notions, however, do not deserve serious consideration, as neither religion nor science has anything to do with unsustainable hypotheses.

The views, moreover, that we expressed in 1849, touching Physical Causes, Congenital Varieties, &c., need no modification at the present day; but, on the contrary, will be found amply sustained by the progress of science, . . .

"Is it not strange that all the remarkable changes of type spoken of by Prichard and others should have occurred in remote antehistoric times, and amongst ignorant erratic tribes? Why is it that no instance of these remarkable changes can be pointed out which admits of conclusive evidence? The civilized nations of Europe have been for many centuries sending colonies to Asia, Africa, and America; amongst Mongols, Malays, Africans, and Indians; and why has no example occurred in any of these colonies to substantiate the argument? The doubtful examples of Prichard are refuted by others, which he cites on the adverse side, of a positive nature. He gives examples of Jews, Persians, Hindoos, Arabs, &c., who have emigrated to foreign climates, and, at the end of one thousand or fifteen hundred years, have preserved their original types in the midst of widely different races. Does nature anywhere operate by such opposite and contradictory laws? . . .

"The unity of the human species has also been stoutly maintained on psychological grounds. Numerous attempts have been made to establish the intellectual equality of the dark races with the white; and the history of the past has been ransacked for examples, but they are nowhere to be found. Can any one call the name of a full-blooded Negro who has ever written a page worthy of being remembered?"

The avowal of the above views drew down upon us, as might have been expected, criticisms more remarkable for virulence of hostility, than for the scientific education of the critics. Our present volume is an evidence that we have survived these transient cavils; and while we have much satisfaction in submitting herein a mass of *facts* that, to the generality of readers in this country, will be surprising, we would remind the theologist, in the language of the very orthodox Hugh Miller (*Footprints of the Creator*), that

> "The clergy, as a class, suffer themselves to linger far in the rear of an intelligent and accomplished laity. Let them not shut their eyes to the danger which is obviously coming. The battle of the evidences of Christianity will have, as certainly to be fought on the field of physical science, as it was contested in the last age on that of the metaphysics."

The Physical history of Man has been likewise trammelled for ages by arbitrary systems of Chronology; more especially by that of the Hebrews, which is now considered, by all competent authorities, as altogether worthless beyond the time of Abraham, and of little value previously to that of Solomon; for it is in his reign that we reach their last positive date. The abandonment of this restricted system is a great point gained; because, instead of being obliged to crowd an immense antiquity, embracing endless details, into a few centuries, we are now free to classify and arrange facts as the requirements of history and science demand.

It is now generally conceded that there exist no data by which we can approximate the date of man's first appearance upon earth; and, for aught we yet know, it may be thousands or millions of years beyond our reach. The spurious systems, of Archbishop Usher on the Hebrew Text, and of Dr. Hales on the Septuagint, being entirely broken down, we turn, unshackled by prejudice, to the monumental records of Egypt as our best guide. Even these soon lose themselves, not in the primitive state of man, but in his middle or perhaps modern ages; for the Egyptian Empire first presents itself to view, about 4000 years before Christ, as that of a mighty nation, in full tide of civilization, and surrounded by other realms and races already emerging from the barbarous stage.

In order that a clear understanding with the reader may be established in the following pages, it becomes necessary to adopt some common standard of chronology for facility of reference.

An esteemed correspondent, Mr. Birch, of the British Museum, aptly observes to us in a private letter—"Although I can see what is *not* the fact in chronology, I have not come to the conclusion of what *is* the truth." Such is precisely our own condition of mind; nor do we suppose that a conscientious student of the subject, as developed under its own head at the close of this volume, can at the present hour obtain, for epochas anterior to Abraham, a solution that must not itself be vague for a century or more. Nevertheless, in Egyptian chronology, we follow the system of Lepsius by assuming the *age of* MENES at B. C. 3893; in Chinese, we accept Pauthier's date for the 1st *historical dynasty* at B. C. 2637; in Assyrian, the results of Layard's last Journey indicate B. C. 1250 as the probable extreme of that country's monumental chronicles; and finally, in Hebrew computation, we agree with Lepsius in deeming Abraham's era to approximate to B. C. 1500. Our *Supplement* offers to the critical reader every facility of verification, with comparative Tables, the repetition of which is here superfluous.

To Egyptology, beyond all question, belongs the honor of dissipating those chronological fables of past generations, continued belief in which, since the recent publication of Chev'r Lepsius's researches, implies simply the credulity of ignorance. One of his letters from the Pyramids of Memphis, in 1843, contained the following almost prophetic passage:

"We are still busy with structures, sculptures, and inscriptions, which are to be classed, by means of the now more accurately-determined groups of kings, in an epoch of highly-flourishing civilization, as far back as the *fourth Millennium before Christ.* We cannot sufficiently impress upon ourselves and others these hitherto incredible dates. The more criticism is provoked by them, and forced to serious examination, the better for the cause. Conviction will soon follow angry criticism; and, finally, those results will be attained, which are so intimately connected with every branch of antiquarian research."

We subscribe without reservation to the above sentiment; and hope we shall not be disappointed in the amount of "angry criticism" which we think the truths embodied in this volume are calculated to provoke. Scientific truth, exemplified in the annals of Astronomy, Geology, Chronology, Geographical distribution of animals, &c., has literally fought its way inch by inch through false theology. The last grand battle between science and dogmatism, on the primitive origin of races, has now commenced. It requires no prophetic eye to foresee that science must again, and finally, triumph.

It may be proper to state, in conclusion, that the subject shall be treated purely as one of science, and that our colleague and ourself will follow facts wherever they may lead, without regard to imaginary consequences. Locally, the "Friend of Moses," no less than other "friends of the Bible" everywhere, have been compelled to make large concessions to science. We shall, in the present investigation, treat the Scriptures simply in their historical and scientific bearings. On former occasions, and in the most respectful manner, we had attempted to conciliate sectarians, and to reconcile the plain teachings of science with theological prejudices; but to no useful purpose. In return, our opinions and motives have been misrepresented and vilified by self-constituted teachers of the Christian religion! We have, in consequence, now done with all this; and no longer have any apologies to offer, nor favors of lenient criticism to ask. The broad banner of science is herein nailed to the mast. Even in our own brief day, we have beheld one flimsy religious dogma after another consigned to oblivon, while science, on the other hand, has been gaining strength and majesty with time. "Nature," says Luke Burke, "has nothing to reveal, that is not noble, and beautiful, and good."

In our former language,

"Man can *invent* nothing in science or religion but falsehood; and all the truths which he *discovers* are but facts or laws which have emanated from the Creator. All science, therefore, may be regarded as a revelation from HIM; and although newly-discovered laws, or facts, in nature, may conflict with religious er-

rors, which have been written and preached for centuries, they never can conflict with religious *truth.* There must be harmony between the works and the words of the Almighty, and wherever they *seem* to conflict, the discord has been produced by the ignorance or wickedness of man."

J. C. N.

MOBILE, *August,* 1853.

SAMUEL CARTWRIGHT (1793-1862)

THE PROGNATHOUS SPECIES
OF MANKIND.

ANOTHER EXPONENT OF THE "scientific" race theory, though not as distinguished a one as Josiah Nott, was Dr. Samuel Cartwright of New Orleans. Whereas Nott was principally concerned with the plural-origins hypothesis, Cartwright tended to take that side of the race argument for granted; he put most of his emphasis on the peculiar characteristics of the Negro as a "species." Cartwright's best-known essay on that subject, first published in the late 1850s and reprinted here, undertakes to describe some of these characteristics and to equate them with a permanently servile relationship toward the white race.

IT IS NOT INTENDED by the use of the term Prognathous to call in question the black man's humanity or the unity of the human races as a *genus*, but to prove that the species of the genus homo are not a unity, but a plurality, each essentially different from the others —one of them being so unlike the other two—the oval-headed Caucasian and the pyramidal-headed Mongolian—as to be actually prognathous, like the brute creation; not that the negro is a brute, or half man and half brute, but a genuine human being, anatomically constructed, about the head and face, more like the monkey tribes and the lower order of animals than any other species of the genus man. Prognathous is a technical term derived from *pro*, before, and *gnathos*, the jaws, indicating that the muzzle or mouth is anterior to the brain. The lower animals, according to Cuvier, are distinguished from the European and Mongol man by the mouth

"Natural History of the Prognathous Species of Mankind," New York *Day-Book*, November 10, 1857; reprinted as Appendix to J. H. Van Evrie, ed., *The Dred Scott Decision: Opinion of Chief Justice Taney* . . . (New York: Van Evrie, Horton & Co., 1859), pp. 45-48; reprinted in E. N. Elliott, *Cotton Is King, and Pro-Slavery Arguments* (Augusta: Pritchard, Abbott & Loomis, 1860), pp. 707-712, 714-716.

and face projecting further forward in the profile than the brain. He expresses the rule thus: *face anterior, cranium posterior.* The typical negroes of adult age, when tried by this rule, are proved to belong to a different species from the man of Europe or Asia, because the head and face are anatomically constructed more after the fashion of the simiadiæ and the brute creation than the Caucasian and Mongolian species of mankind, their mouth and jaws projecting beyond the forehead containing the anterior lobes of the brain. Moreover, their faces are proportionally larger than their crania, instead of smaller, as in the other two species of the genus man. Young monkeys and young negroes, however, are not prognathous like their parents, but become so as they grow older. The head of the infant ourang outang is like that of a well formed Caucasian child in the projection and height of the forehead and the convexity of the vertea. The brain appears to be larger than it really is, because the face, at birth, has not attained its proportional size. The face of the Caucasian infant is a little under its proportional size when compared with the cranium. In the infant negro and ourang outang it is greatly so. Although so much smaller in infancy than the cranium, the face of the young monkey ultimately outgrows the cranium; so, also, does the face of the young negro, whereas in the Caucasian, the face always continues to be smaller than the cranium. The superfices of the face at puberty exceeds that of the hairy scalp both in the negro and the monkey, while it is always less in the white man. Young monkeys and young negroes are superior to white children of the same age in memory and other intellectual faculties. The white infant comes into the world with its brain inclosed by fifteen disunited bony plates—the occipital bone being divided into four parts, the sphenoid into three, the frontal into two, each of the two temporals into two, which, with the two parietals, make fifteen plates in all—the vomer and ethmoid not being ossified at birth. The bones of the head are not only disunited, but are more or less overlapped at birth, in consequence of the largeness of the Caucasian child's head and the smallness of its mother's pelvis, giving the head an elongated form, and an irregular, knotty feel to the touch. The negro infant, however, is born with a small, hard, smooth, round head like a gourd. Instead of the frontal and temporal bones being divided into six plates, as in the white child, they form but one bone in the negro infant. The head is not only smaller than that of the white child, but the pelvis of the negress is wider than that of the white woman—its greater obliquity also favors parturition and prevents miscarriage.

Negro children and white children are alike at birth in one remarkable particular—they are both born *white*, and so much alike, as far as color is concerned, as scarcely to be distinguished from each other. In a very short time, however, the skin of the negro infant begins to darken and continues to grow darker until it becomes of a shining black color, provided the child be healthy. The skin will become black whether exposed to the air and light or not. The blackness is not of as deep a shade during the first years of life, as afterward. The black color is not so deep in the female as in the male, nor in the feeble, sickly negro as in the robust and healthy. Blackness is a characteristic of the prognathous species of the genus homo, but all the varieties of all the prognathous species are not equally black. Nor are the individuals of the same family or variety equally so. The lighter shades of color, when not derived from admixture with Mongolian or Caucasian blood, indicate degeneration in the prognathous species. The Hottentots, Bushmen and aborigines of Australia are inferior in mind and body to the typical African of Guinea and the Niger.

The typical negroes themselves are more or less superior or inferior to one another precisely as they approximate to or recede from the typical standard in color and form, due allowance being made for age and sex. The standard is an oily, shining black, and as far as the conformation of the head and face is concerned and the relative proportion of nervous matter outside of the cranium to the quantity of cerebral matter within it, is found between the simiadiae and the Caucasian. Thus, in the typical negro, a perpendicular line, let fall from the forehead, cuts off a large portion of the face, throwing the mouth, the thick lips, and the projecting teeth anterior to the cranium, but not the entire face, as in the lower animals and monkey tribes. When all, or a greater part of the face is thrown anterior to the line, the negro approximates the monkey anatomically more than he does the true Caucasian; and when little or

none of the face is anterior to the line, he approximates that myth-
ical being of Dr. Van Evrie, *a black white man*, and almost ceases
to be a negro. The black man occasionally seen in Africa, called the
Bature Dutu, with high nose, thin lips, and long straight hair, is not
a negro at all, but a Moor tanned by the climate—because his
children, not exposed to the sun, do not become black like himself.
The typical negro's nervous system is modeled a little different from
the Caucasian and somewhat like the ourang outang. The medullary
spinal cord is larger and more developed than in the white man, but
less so than in the monkey tribes. The occipital foramen, giving
exit to the spinal cord, is a third longer, says Cuvier, in proportion
to its breadth, than in the Caucasian, and is so oblique as to form an
angle of 30° with the horizon, yet not so oblique as in the simiadiae,
but sufficiently so to throw the head somewhat backward and the
face upward in the erect position. Hence, from the obliquity of the
head and the pelvis, the negro walks steadier with a weight on his
head, as a pail of water for instance, than without it; whereas, the
white man, with a weight on his head, has great difficulty in maintaining his centre of gravity, owing to the occipital foramen forming no angle with the cranium, the pelvis, the spine, or the thighs—
all forming a straight line from the crown of the head to the sole
of the foot without any of the obliquities seen in the negro's knees,
thighs, pelvis and head—and still more evident in the ourang
outang.

The nerves of organic life are larger in the prognathous species
of mankind than in the Caucasian species, but not so well developed as in the simiadiæ. The brain is about a tenth smaller in
the prognathous man than in the Frenchman, as proved by actual
measurement of skulls by the French savants, Palisot and Virey.
Hence, from the small brain and the larger nerves, the digestion
of the prognathous species is better than that of the Caucasian, and
its animal appetites stronger, approaching the simiadiæ but stop-
ping short of their beastiality. The nostrils of the prognathous
species of mankind open higher up than they do in the white or
olive species, but not so high up as in the monkey tribes. In the
gibbon, for instance, they open between the orbits. Although the
typical negro's nostrils open high up, yet owing to the nasal bones

being short and flat, there is no projection or prominence formed between his orbits by the bones of the nose, as in the Caucasian species. The nostrils, however, are much wider, about as wide from wing to wing, as the white man's mouth from corner to corner, and the internal bones, called the turbinated, on which the olfactory nerves are spread, are larger and project nearer to the opening of the nostrils than in the white man. Hence the negro approximates the lower animals in his sense of smell, and can detect snakes by that sense alone. All the senses are more acute, but less delicate and discriminating, than the white man's. He has a good ear for melody but not for harmony, a keen taste and relish for food but less discriminating between the different kinds of esculent substances than the Caucasian. His lips are immensely thicker than any of the white race, his nose broader and flatter, his chin smaller and more retreating, his foot flatter, broader, larger, and the heel longer, while he has scarcely any calves at all to his legs when compared to an equally healthy and muscular white man. He does not walk flat on his feet but on the outer sides, in consequence of the sole of the foot having a direction inwards, from the legs and thighs being arched outwards and the knees bent. The verb, from which his Hebrew name is derived, points out this flexed position of the knees, and also clearly expresses the servile type of his mind. Ham, the father of Canaan, when translated into plain English, reads that a black man was the father of the slave or knee-bending species of mankind.

The blackness of the prognathous race, known in the world's history as Canaanites, Cushites, Ethiopians, black men or negroes, is not confined to the skin, but pervades, in a greater or less degree, the whole inward man down to the bones themselves, giving the flesh and the blood, the membranes and every organ and part of the body, except the bones, a darker hue than in the white race. Who knows but what Canaan's mother may have been a genuine Cushite, as black inside as out, and that Cush, which means blackness, was the mark put upon Cain? Whatever may have been the mark set upon Cain, the negro, in all ages of the world, has carried with him a mark equally efficient in preventing him from being slain—the mark of blackness. The wild Arabs and hostile American Indians invariably catch the black wanderer and make a slave of him instead of killing him, as they do the white man.

Nich. Pechlin, in a work written last century entitled "De cute Athiopum," Albinus, in another work, entitled "De sede et causa coloris Athiop," as also the great German anatomists, Meiners, Ebel, and Soemmering, all bear witness to the fact that the muscles, blood, membranes, and all the internal organs of the body, (the bones alone excepted,) are of a darker hue in the negro than in the white man. They estimate the difference in color to be equal to that which exists between the hare and the rabbit. Who ever doubts the fact, or has none of those old and impartial authorities at hand—impartial because they were written before England adopted the policy of pressing religion and science in her service to place white American republican freemen and Guinea negroes upon the same platform—has only to look into the mouth of the first healthy typical negro he meets to be convinced of the truth, that the entire membraneous lining of the inside of the cheeks, lips and gums is of à much darker color than in the white man.

The negro, however, must be healthy and in good condition—sickness, hard usage and chronic ailments, particularly that cachexia, improperly called consumption, speedily extracts the coloring matter out of the mucous membranes, leaving them paler and whiter than in the Caucasian. The bleaching process of bad health or degeneration begins in the blood, membranes and muscles, and finally extracts so much of the coloring pigment out of the skin, as to give it a dull ashy appearance, sometimes extracting the whole of it, converting the negro into the albino. Albinoism or cucosis does not necessarily imply hybridism. It occurs among the pure Africans from any cause producing a degeneration of the species. Hybridism, however, is the most prolific source of that degeneration. Sometimes the degeneration shows itself by white spots, like the petals of flowers, covering different parts of the skin. The Mexicans are subject to a similar degeneration, only that the spots and stripes are black instead of white. It is called the pinto with them. Even the pigment of the iris and the coloring matter of the albino's hair is absorbed, giving it a silvery white appearance, and converting him into a clairvoyant at night. According to Professors Brown, Seidy and Gibbs, the negro's hair is not tubular, like the white man's, but it is eccentrically elliptical, with flattened edges, the coloring matter residing in the epidermis, and not in tubes. In the place of a tube, the shaft of each hair is surrounded with a scaly covering like sheep's wool, and, like wool, is capable of being felted. True hair does not possess that property. The degeneration called albinoism has a remarkable influence upon the hair, destroying its coarse, nappy, wooly appearance, and converting it into fine, long, soft, silky, curly threads. Often, the whole external skin, so remarkably void of hair in the healthy negro, becomes covered with a very fine, silky down, scarcely perceptible to the naked eye, when transformed into the albino. . . .

Mr. Bowen [a South Carolina Baptist who served from 1849 to 1856 as a missionary in Central Africa] inferred that the negroes of Central Africa, although diminishing in numbers, are rising higher in the scale of humanity, from the very small circumstance that they do not emit from their bodies so strong and so offensive an odor as the negro slaves of Georgia and the Carolinas do, nor are their skins of so deep a black. This is a good illustration of the important truth, that all the danger of the slavery question lies in the ignorance of Scripture and the natural history of the negro. A little acquaintance with the negro's natural history would prove to Mr. Bowen that the strong odor emitted by the negro, like the deep pigment of the skin, is an indication of high health, happiness, and good treatment, while its deficiency is a sure sign of unhappiness, disease, bad treatment, or degeneration. The skin of a happy, healthy negro is not only blacker and more oily than an unhappy, unhealthy one, but emits the strongest odor when the body is warmed by exercise and the soul is filled with the most pleasurable emotions. In the dance called *patting juber*, the odor emitted from the men, intoxicated with pleasure, is often so powerful as to throw the negro women into paroxysms of unconsciousness, vulgo hysterics. On another point of much importance there is no practical difference between the Rev. missionary and that clear-headed, bold, and eccentric old Methodist, Dr. McFarlane. Both believe that the Bible can do ignorant, sensual savages no good; both believe that nothing but compulsatory power can restrain uncivilized barbarians from polygamy, inebriety, and other sinful practices.

The good missionary, however, believes in the possibility of civilizing the inferior races by the money and means of the Christian nations lavishly bestowed, after which he thinks it will be no difficult matter to convert them to Christianity. Whereas the venerable Methodist believes in the impossibility of civilizing them, and therefore concludes that the Written Word was not intended for those inferior races who can not read it. When the philosophy of the prognathous species of mankind is better understood, it will be seen how they, the lowest of the human species, can be made partakers, equally with the highest, in the blessings and benefits of the Written Word of God. The plantation laws against polygamy, intoxicating drinks, and other besetting sins of the negro race in the savage state, are gradually and silently converting the African barbarian into a moral, rational, and civilized being, thereby rendering the heart a fit tabernacle for the reception of Gospel truths. The prejudices of many, perhaps the majority of the Southern people, against educating the negroes they hold in subjection, arise from some vague and indefinite fears of its consequences, suggested by the abolition and British theories built on the false assumption that the negro is a white man with a black skin. If such an assumption had the smallest degree of truth in it, the more profound the ignorance and the deeper sunk in barbarism the slaves were kept, the better it would be for them and their masters. But experience proves that masters and overseers have nothing at all to fear from civilized and intelligent negroes, and no trouble whatever in managing them—that all the trouble, insubordination and danger arise from the uncivilized, immoral, rude, and grossly ignorant portion of the servile race. It is not the ignorant semi-barbarian that the master or overseer intrusts with his keys, his money, his horse or his gun, but the most intelligent of the plantation—one whose intellect and morals have undergone the best training. An educated negro, one whose intellect and morals have been cultivated, is worth double the price of the wild, uncultivated, black barbarian of Cuba and will do twice as much work, do it better and with less trouble.

The prejudice against educating the negroes may also be traced to the neglect of American divines in making themselves acquainted with Hebrew literature. What little the most of them know of the meaning of the untranslated terms occurring in the Bible, and the signification of the verbs from which they are derived, is mostly gathered from British commentators and glossary-makers, who have blinked the facts that disprove the Exeter Hall dogma, that negro slavery is sin against God. Hence, even in the South, the important Biblical truth, that the white man derives his authority to govern the negro from the Great Jehovah, is seldom proclaimed from the pulpit. If it were proclaimed, the master race would see deeper into their responsibilities, and look closer into the duties they owe to the people whom God has given them as an inheritance, and their children after them, so long as time shall last. That man has no faith in the Scriptures who believes that education could defeat God's purposes, in subjecting the black man to the government of the white. On the contrary, experience proves its advantages, to both parties. Aside and apart from Scripture authority, natural history reveals most of the same facts, in regard to the negro that the Bible does. It proves the existence of at least three distinct species of the genus man, differing in their instincts, form, habits and color. The white species having qualities denied to the black—one with a free and the other with a servile mind—one a thinking and reflective being, the other a creature of feeling and imitation, almost void of reflective faculties, and consequently unable to provide for and take care of himself. The relation of master and slave would naturally spring up between two such different species of men, even if there was no Scripture authority to support it. The relation thus established, being natural, would be drawn closer together, instead of severed, by the inferior imitating the superior in all his ways, or in other words, acquiring an education.

NEHEMIAH ADAMS (1806-1878)

A SOUTH-SIDE VIEW OF SLAVERY.

THE FOLLOWING PASSAGE, written in 1854, was not intended by its author as part of the pro-slavery argument. Yet its effect upon anti-slavery opinion could not have been other than subversive, and it supplied an element which, in some form, the South found indispensable in maintaining its moral position: it pictured the decent side of plantation slavery. From a Southern viewpoint, moreover, the author himself was too good to be true.

Nehemiah Adams was a Boston minister whose health required him in 1853 to spend three months in the South. He had had strong anti-slavery leanings, and the last thing he did before leaving home was to sign a remonstrance, which he himself had helped to frame, against the contemplated extension of slavery into Kansas and Nebraska. What he saw of slavery in Georgia, South Carolina, and Virginia, however, caused him to reverse a number of his opinions. He was unprepared to find slaveholders who were human beings like himself; he was deeply impressed by the benign scenes of plantation life which he witnessed; and he came away with a heightened sense of sympathy for the South and its institutions. The book he wrote upon his return, *A South-Side View of Slavery,* gives a full account of this experience. The following chapter describes a slave sale, and in the process shows how even the worst side of Southern slavery could be mitigated in practice by the better instincts of Southern society.

SECTION I.—Slave Auctions.

PASSING UP THE STEPS of a court-house in a southern town with some gentlemen, I saw a man sitting on the steps with a colored infant, wrapped in a coverlet, its face visible, and the child asleep.

It is difficult for some who have young children not to bestow a passing look or salutation upon a child; but besides this, the sight before me seemed out of place and strange.

"Is the child sick?" I said to the man, as I was going up the steps.

"No, master; she is going to be sold."

A South-Side View of Slavery (Boston: T. R. Marvin & B. B. Mussey, 1854), pp. 64-81.

"Sold! Where is her mother?"

"At home, master."

"How old is the child?"

"She is about a year, master."

"You are not selling the child, of course. How comes she here?"

"I don't know, master; only the sheriff told me to sit down here and wait till twelve o'clock, sir."

It is hardly necessary to say that my heart died within me. Now I had found slavery in its most awful feature—the separation of a child from its mother.

"The mother is at home, master." What are her feelings? What were they when she missed the infant? Was it taken openly, or by stealth? Who has done this? What shape, what face had he? The mother is not dead; "the mother is at home, master." What did they do to you, Rachel, weeping and refusing to be comforted?

Undetermined whether I would witness the sale, whether I could trust myself in such a scene, I walked into a friend's law office, and looked at his books. I heard the sheriff's voice, the "public outcry," as the vendue is called, but did not go out, partly because I would not betray the feelings which I knew would be awakened.

One of my friends met me a few minutes after, who had witnessed the transaction.

"You did not see the sale," he said.

"No. Was the child sold?"

"Yes, for one hundred and forty dollars."

I could take this case, so far as I have described it, go into any pulpit or upon any platform at the north, and awaken the deepest emotions known to the human heart, harrow up the feelings of every father and mother, and make them pass a resolution surcharged with all the righteous indignation which language can express. All that any speaker who might have preceded me, supposing the meeting to be one for discussion, might have said respecting the contentment, good looks, happy relations of the slaves, I could have rendered of no avail to his argument by this little incident. No matter what kindness may be exercised in ten thousand instances;

a system in which the separation of an infant from its mother is an essential element can not escape reprobation.

On relating what I had seen to some southern ladies, they became pale with emotion; they were silent; they were filled with evident distress. But before remarking upon this case, I will give another. My attention was arrested by the following advertisement:—

"Guardian's Sale.

"Will be sold before the court-house door in ——, on the first Tuesday in May next, agreeably to an order of the ordinary of —— county, the interest of the minors of ——, in a certain negro girl named ——, said interest being three fourths of said negro."

Three fourths of a negro girl to be sold at auction! There was something here which excited more than ordinary curiosity: the application of vulgar fractions to personal identity was entirely new. I determined to witness this sale.

An hour before the appointed time, I saw the girl sitting alone on the steps of the court-house. She wore a faded but tidy orange-colored dress, a simple handkerchief on her head, and she was barefoot. Her head was resting upon her hand, with her elbow on her knee. I stood unperceived and looked at her. Poor, lonely thing, waiting to be sold on the steps of that court-house! The place of justice is a bleak promontory, from which you look off as upon a waste of waters—a dreary, shoreless waste. What avails every mitigation of slavery? Had I become a convert to the system, here is enough to counterbalance all my good impressions.

The sheriff arrived at noon, and the people assembled. The purchaser was to have the services of the girl three fourths of the time, a division of property having given some one a claim to one fourth of her appraised value.

The girl was told to stand up. She had a tall, slender form, and was, in all respects, an uncommonly good-looking child.

The bidding commenced at two hundred dollars, and went on in an animated and exciting manner.

The girl began to cry, and wiped her tears with the back of her

hand; no one replied to her; the bidding went on; she turned her
back to the people. I saw her shoulders heave with her suppressed
crying; she said something in a confused voice to a man who sat
behind the auctioneer.

When I was young I was drawn, by mingling with some older
schoolmates, strongly against my will, and every moment purposing
an escape, to see a youth executed for arson. I resolved that I
would never look upon such a sight again. But here I was behold-
ing something which moved me as I had not been moved for all
these long years.

She was fourteen years old. A few days before I had sent to a
child of mine, entering her fourteenth year, a birthday gift. By
this coincidence I was led to think of this slave girl with some
peculiar feelings. I made the case my own. She was a child to
parents, living or dead, whose hearts, unless perverted by some unnatural process, would yearn over her and be distracted by this
sight.

Four hundred and forty-five dollars was the last bid, and the
man sitting behind the sheriff said to her kindly, "Well, run and
jump into the wagon."

A large number of citizens had assembled to witness the sale of
this girl; some of them men of education and refinement, humane
and kind. On any question of delicacy and propriety, in every thing
related to the finest sentiments, I would have felt it a privilege to
learn of them. How then, I said to myself as I watched their faces,
can you look upon a scene like this as upon an ordinary business
transaction, when my feelings are so tumultuous, and all my sensibilities are excruciated? You are not hard-hearted men; you are
gentle and generous. In my intercourse with you I have often felt,
in the ardor of new friendships, how happy I should be to have
you in my circle of immediate friends at home; what ornaments
you would be to any circle of Christian friends. Some of you are
graduates of Yale College; some of Brown University: you know
all that I know about the human heart: I hesitate to believe that
I am right and you wrong. If to sell a human being at auction
were all which I feel it to be, you must know it as well as I. Yet
I cannot yield my convictions. Why do we differ so in our feel-

ings? Instances of private humanity and tenderness have satisfied
me that you would not lay one needless burden upon a human
being, nor see him suffer without redress. Is it because you are
used to the sight that you endure it with composure? or because
it is an essential part of a system which you groan under but cannot remove?

To begin with the sale of the infant. During my stay in the
place, three or four estimable gentlemen said to me, each in private,
"I understand that you saw that infant sold the other day. We are
very sorry that you happened to see it. Nothing of the kind ever
took place before to our knowledge, and we all feared that it would
make an unhappy impression upon you."

The manner in which this was said affected me almost as much
as the thing which had given occasion to it. Southern hearts and
consciences, I felt reassured, were no more insensible than mine.
The system had not steeled the feelings of these gentlemen; the
presence of a northerner, a friend, retaining his private, natural
convictions, as they perceived, without unkindness of words or
manner, made them·look at the transaction with his eyes; every
kind and generous emotion was alive in their hearts; they felt
that such a transaction needed to be explained and justified.

How could they explain it? How could they justify it? With
many, if not with all of my readers, it is a foregone conclusion,
as it had been with me, that the case admits of no explanation or
justification.

I received, as I said, three or four statements with regard to
the case, and this is the substance of them:—

The mother of this infant belonged to a man who had become
embarrassed in his circumstances, in consequence of which the
mother was sold to another family in the same place, before the
birth of the child; but the first owner still laid claim to the child,
and there was some legal doubt with regard to his claim. He was
disposed to maintain this claim, and it became a question how the
child should be taken from him. A legal gentleman, whose name is
familiar to the country, told me that he was consulted, and he ad-
vised that through an old execution the child should be levied
upon, be sold at auction, and thus be removed from him. The plan

succeeded. The child was attached, advertised, and offered for sale. The mother's master bought it, at more than double the ratable price, and the child went to its mother.

Nor was this all. In the company of bidders there was a man employed by a generous lady to attend the sale, and see that the infant was restored to its mother. The lady had heard that the sale was to take place, but did not fully know the circumstances, and her purpose was to prevent the child from passing from the parent. Accordingly her agent and the agent of the mother's master were bidding against each other for some time, each with the same benevolent determination to restore the child to its mother.

Rachel was comforted. Rather she had had no need of being comforted, for the sheriff was in this case to be her avenger and protector. Here was slavery restoring a child to its mother; here was a system which can deal in unborn children, redressing its own wrong. Moreover, the law which forbids the sale of a child under five years was violated, in order to keep the child with its mother. Some other points might be stated, but the accounts respecting them differed.

Had I not known the sequel of the story, what a thrilling, effective appeal could I have made at the north by the help of this incident. Then what injustice I should have inflicted upon the people of that place; what stimulus might I have given to the rescue of a fugitive slave; what resuscitation to the collapsing vocabulary of epithets. How might I have helped on the dissolution of the Union; how have led half our tribes to swear that they would have war with the rest forever, when in truth the men and women who had done this thing had performed one of the most tender and humane actions, and did prevent, and, if necessary, with their earthly all, (for I knew them well,) would have prevented that from ever taking place to which, in my ignorance and passion, I should have sworn that I could bear witness—an infant taken from its mother's breast and sold.

The "three fourths" of the girl were bought by the owner of the other fourth, who already had possession of her. The sale took place that he might be her sole owner. That word which followed the sale, "Well, run and jump into the wagon," was music to the child.

I understood afterward why she turned her back to the crowd, and looked at the man who sat behind the sheriff. He was her master, and he owned her mother; the girl heard the bidding from the company, and heard her master bidding; the conflict she understood; she was at stake, as she felt, for life; it took some time for the bidding to reach four hundred dollars; hope deferred made her heart sick; she turned and kept her eye on her master, to see whether he would suffer himself to be defeated. He sat quietly using his knife upon a stick, like one whose mind was made up; the result of the sale in his favor excited no new feeling in him; but the ready direction, "Well, run and jump into the wagon," was as much as to say, I have done what I meant to do when I came here.

I did not see "Jacob," forty-five years of age, well recommended, who was advertised to be sold at the same time and place. The sheriff announced that the sale of Jacob was merely to perfect a title. There was only one bid, therefore—six hundred dollars; the owner thus going through a form to settle some legal question.

We are all ready to inquire as to the views and feelings of good men at the south with regard to the sale of slaves at auction. I felt great curiosity to know how some of the best of men regarded it.

1. They say that very many of the slaves advertised with full descriptions, looking like invitations to buy, are merely legal appointments to determine claims, settle estates, without any purpose to let the persons offered for sale pass from the families to which they belong.

It was some relief to know as much as this. At home and at the south advertisements in southern papers of negroes for sale at auction, describing them minutely, have often harrowed our feelings. The minute description, they say, is, or may be, a legal defence in the way of proof and identification.

2. However trying a public sale may be to the feelings of the slave, they say that it is for his interest that the sale should be public.

The sale of slaves at auction in places where they are known—and this is the case every where except in the largest cities—excites deep interest in some of the citizens of that place. They are drawn to the sale with feelings of personal regard for the slaves, and are vigilant to prevent unprincipled persons from purchasing and carrying them away, and even from possessing them in their own neighborhood. I know of citizens combining to prevent such men from buying, and of their contributing to assist good men and women in purchasing the servants at prices greatly increased by such competition. In all such cases the law requiring and regulating public sales and advertisements of sales prevents those private transfers which would defeat the good intentions of benevolent men. It is an extremely rare case for a servant or servants who have been known in town to be removed into hands which the people of the place generally would not approve.

The sale of a negro at public auction is not a reckless, unfeeling thing in the towns at the south, where the subjects of the sale are from among themselves. In settling estates, good men exercise as much care with regard to the disposition of the slaves as though they were providing homes for white orphan children; and that too when they have published advertisements of slaves in such connections with horses and cattle, that, when they are read by a northerner, his feelings are excruciated. In hearing some of the best of men, such as are found in all communities, largely intrusted with the settlement of estates, men of extreme fairness and incorruptible integrity, speak of the word "chattel" as applied to slaves, it is obvious that this unfeeling law term has no counterpart in their minds, nor in the feelings of the community in general.

Slaves are allowed to find masters and mistresses who will buy them. Having found them, the sheriffs' and administrators' sales must by law be made public, the persons must be advertised, and every thing looks like an unrestricted offer, while it is the understanding of the company that the sale has really been made in private.

Sitting in the reading-room of a hotel one morning, I saw a colored woman enter and courtesy to a gentleman opposite.

"Good morning, sir. Please, sir, how is Ben?"

"Ben—he is very well. But I don't know you."

"Ben is my husband. I heard you were in town, and I want you to buy me. My mistress is dead these three weeks, and the family is to be broken up."

"Well, I will buy you. Where shall I inquire?"

All this was said and done in as short a time as it takes to read it; but this woman was probably obliged by law, in the settlement of the estate, to be advertised and described.

All these things go far to mitigate our feelings with regard to the sale of slaves at auction in many cases. But even with regard to these cases, no one who is not used to the sight will ever see it but with repugnance and distress.

I walked with a gentleman, esteemed and honored by his fellow-citizens, and much intrusted with the settlement of estates. I knew that he would appreciate my feelings, and I disclosed them. I asked him if there were no other way of changing the relations of slaves in process of law, except by exposing them, male and female, at auction, on the court-house steps. I told him how I felt on seeing the girl sold, and that the knowledge subsequently of the satisfactory manner in which the case was disposed of did not make me cease to feel unhappy. I could not bear to see a fellow-being made a subject of sale, even in form; and I wondered that any one could look upon it with composure, or suffer it to be repeated without efforts to abolish it.

His reply was, for substance, that so far as he and the people of his town were concerned, no case of hardship in the disposal of a slave had ever occurred there, to his knowledge; that he had settled a large number of estates, and in every case had disposed of the servants in ways satisfactory to themselves; that he had prevented certain men from bidding upon them; that he had prevailed on others not to buy, because he and the servants were unwilling to have these men for their masters; and, therefore, that the question was practically reduced to the expediency of the form of transfer, viz., by public vendue.

He repeated what I have said of the desirableness that the sale or transfer should be public; whether in a room, or on steps, was unimportant, only that every public outcry was ordained to be made at the court-house. He also said that the slaves, knowing that the sale was a mere form, and that they were already disposed of, did not in such cases suffer to the degree which strangers supposed. It was evident, from all that he said, that he transfused his own kind, benevolent feelings, and those of his fellow-citizens over every sale within the limits of his town, and could not, therefore, see it with a northerner's eyes and heart.

The forms of law are as inconsiderate of our feelings as though they were acts of barbarians. A sheriff's sale of house furniture in the dwelling of a man who has fallen from opulence into insolvency is like the wheel of torture, that breaks every bone and joint one by one. The auctioneer, with precious household treasures, keepsakes, memorials of dear departed friends, in one hand, and a crumpled newspaper for a hammer in the other, seems to be a most unfeeling man; but he is not so; it is law, of which he is the exponent, that is so terrible.

No human being, innocent of crime, ought to be subjected to the rack of being offered for sale, nor ought fellow-creatures ever to behold that sight. It will be done away. Reproachful words, however, will not hasten the removal of it.

I once stated the subject to a friend in this form: We cannot expect that servants can abide in a house forever. Death breaks up their relations, and they must have other masters. Allowing all you say of their being necessarily a serving class, why not always give them a voice in changing these relations? This is done uniformly in some of your towns. I could name one in which no slave has been disposed of otherwise for ten years at least, except in cases of refractory and troublesome persons.

Then let opportunity be given for private inquiry and examination; let the transfer be made without obliging the slave to be present, and this will approximate as far as possible to the method of obtaining servants at employment offices.

At the Christmas holidays, some of the southern cities and towns are alive with the negroes, in their best attire, seeking employment for the year to come, changing places, and having full liberty to suit themselves as to their employers. The characters and habits of all the masters and mistresses are known and freely discussed by them.

So, instead of selling a family at auction upon the death of a

master, it is often the case that letters are written for them to
people in different States, where they may happen to have ac-
quaintances, perhaps to relatives of the master's family, known
and beloved, asking them to buy; and thus the family is disposed
of to the satisfaction of all concerned. Wherever kindness prevails,
the evils of slavery can be made to disappear as much as from any
condition, especially where the servants are worthy.

But then there are cases in which the feelings of the slave are
wantonly disregarded, and the owners make no distinction, and are
incapable of making any, between a negro and a mule.

Then there are slaves who are vicious and disagreeable, whom
their owners are glad to sell out of their sight, as other men are
glad to be rid of certain apprentices or refractory children, and
feel happier the greater the distance to which they remove.

Again, men in pecuniary straits, in the hands of a broker or
sheriff, do things which excruciate themselves as much as their
slaves. Thus, in part, the domestic slave trade is maintained.

SECTION II.—*Domestic Slave Trade.*

A southern physician described to me a scene in the domestic
slave trade. He touched at a landing-place in a steamer, and immediately a slave coffle was marched on board. Men, women, and
children, about forty in all, two by two, an ox chain passing through
the double file, and a fastening reaching from the right and left
hands of those on either side of the chain, composed what is called
a *slave coffle.* Some colored people were on the wharf, who seemed
to be relatives and friends of the gang. Such shrieks, such unearthly
noises, as resounded above the escape of steam, my informant said
can not be described. There were partings for life, and between
what degrees of kindred the nature of the cries were probably a sign.

When the boat was on her way, my informant fell into conversation with a distinguished planter, with regard to the scene
which they had just witnessed. They deplored it as one of the
features of a system which they both mourned over, and wished to
abolish, or at least correct, till no wrong, no pain, should be the
fruit of it which is not incidental to every human lot.

While they were discussing the subject, the slave-dealer heard their talk, came up, and made advances to shake hands with the planter. The gentleman drew back, and said, "Sir, I consider you a disgrace to human nature." He poured scorn and indignation upon him.

He spoke the feelings of the south generally. Negro traders are the abhorrence of all flesh. Even their descendants, when they are known, and the property acquired in the traffic, have a blot upon them. I never knew a deeper aversion to any class of men; it is safe to say, that generally it is not surpassed by our feelings toward foreign slave traders.

They go into the States where the trade is not prohibited by law, find men who are in want of money, or a master who has a slave that is troublesome, and for the peace of the plantation that slave is sold, sometimes at great sacrifice; and there are many of whom, under pecuniary pressure, it is not always difficult to purchase.

There are some men whose diabolical natures are gratified by this traffic—passionate, cruel, tyrannical men, seeking dominion in some form to gratify these instincts. The personal examinations which they make, and the written descriptions which they give, of slaves whom they buy, are sometimes disgusting in the extreme. It is beyond explanation that good men at the south do not clamor against this thing, till the transfer of every human being, if he must be a slave, is made with all the care attending the probate of a will.

The charge of vilely multiplying negroes in Virginia, is one of those exaggerations of which this subject is full, and is reduced to this—that Virginia, being an old State, fully stocked, the surplus black population naturally flows off where their numbers are less.

I heard this conversation at the breakfast house of a southern railroad. As several of us were warming ourselves at the fire, one of the passengers said to the keeper of the house,—

"Where is Alonzo now?"

"He is in Alabama."

"I thought he had come back."

"Well, he was to come back some time ago; but they keep sending him so many negroes to sell, he can't leave."

Alonzo is probably a negro trader of the better sort; a mere agent or factor. If slaves are to be sold, there must be men to negotiate with regard to them; these are not all of the vilest sort; yet their occupation is abhorred.

The separation of families seems to be an inevitable feature of slavery, as it exists at present. If a man is rich and benevolent, he will provide for his servants, and tax himself to support them, let their number be never so great, buying one plantation after another, chiefly to employ his people. But the time will come when he must die, and his people are deprived of his protection. No one child, perhaps, can afford to keep them together; perhaps he has no children; then they must take their chance of separations to the widest borders of the slave States. But here individual kindness mitigates sorrow and distress. The owner of several plantations at the south, with no children, has made his slaves his heirs, on condition that they remove to Liberia.

It seems to be taken for granted that to be sold is inevitably to pass from a good to an inferior condition. This is as much a mistake as it would be to assert the same of changes on the part of domestic servants in the free States. There are as good masters as those whose death makes it necessary to scatter the slaves of an estate. The change itself is not necessarily an evil.

We must remember that slaves are not the only inhabitants, nor slave families the only families, in the land, that are scattered by the death of others. Sometimes the demand seems to be that slaves should be kept together at all events, and separations never be permitted. This is absurd, upon the least reflection. No one ought to demand or expect for them an experience better or worse than the common lot of men. Let the slaves share with us in the common blessings and calamities of divine providence. What would become of our families of five or ten children should their parents die? Can we keep our children about us always? Do none but black children go to the ends of the Union and become settled there? How many white people there are that do this, who—deplorable truth!—cannot read and write, and seldom if ever hear of their relatives from whom they are separated. Let us not require too much of slavery. Let us not insist that the slaves shall never be separated, nor their families broken up; but let it be done as in the course of nature every where, with no more pain, nor pain of any other kind, than must accrue to those who depend upon their own efforts for a living.

Facts connected with this part of the subject have given me deep respect and sympathy for those slaveholders who, from the number of instances which have come to my knowledge, it is evident are by no means few, that suffer hardship and loss in their efforts to keep the members of their slave families together. Our knowledge of distressing cases, and the indisputable truth that slavery gives the power of disposal to the owner at his will, no doubt leads us to exaggerate the number of cases in which suffering is unjustly inflicted. While we are sure to hear of distressing cruelties, ten thousand acts of kindness are not mentioned. These can not compensate, however, for the liability to abuse which there is in authority almost absolute; but still let us discriminate when we bring charges against a whole community, and let us consider how far the evils complained of are inseparable, not only from a system which is felt to be a burden, but also from human nature in every condition.

As was remarked with regard to sales by auction, it is in vain to expect that painful separations of families in a wanton manner, or by stress of circumstances, can wholly cease, in the present system. It is indeed a burdensome system, destroying itself by its own weight, unless relieved by some of those unnatural and violent expedients. It is deplored for this and other reasons by multitudes at the south, whose voices we shall hear as soon as our relations as north and south are such as will allow them to speak. In the mean time, public sentiment is fast correcting abuses under the system; and not only so, but through its influence and the power of Christian love, the condition of families and individuals among the slaves is becoming here and there as free from evil as human nature permits in a dependent condition.

EDWARD A. POLLARD (1831-1872)

BLACK DIAMONDS.

ANOTHER EFFORT, descriptive rather than theoretical, to exhibit Negro slavery as one of the mellowest features of Southern life, was a volume of sketches published in 1859 by the Virginia journalist Edward A. Pollard. This same writer was to gain considerable attention after the war for his *Lost Cause* (1866) and *Lost Cause Regained* (1868).

Black Diamonds was arranged in the form of letters to a certain "C.," a Northern acquaintance who was presumably awaiting enlightenment on the true condition of the Negro slave. With an edginess not fully consistent with his theme, Pollard declares that the Southern Negro is the most lovable of creatures—"in his place"—to those who truly know and understand him. His happy state, a state of perpetual irresponsible childhood, would be inconceivable under any other social system than that in which he now functions.

Two of the myths allegedly created by Northern propaganda—those involving the dignified Christianity of "Uncle Tom" and the heart-rending pathos of the slave auction—are challenged in the following excerpt.

IN WRITING TO YOU, my dear C., of the South and its *peculiar institution* (as I intend), I am sure that I have no prejudice to dispel from your mind on the subject; but as I may hereafter publish some extracts from the correspondence, I hope the sketches, which may amuse you, may correct the false views of others, derived, as they chiefly are, from the libels of Northern spies, who live or travel here in disguise. Thus I observed lately a communication in some of the Abolition papers, professing to have been written by one who has been a resident of Macon for eleven years, to the effect that the people here do not allow Northern papers to circulate or be taken by subscribers, or even Congressional documents to be among them, which do not harmonize with their peculiar views. Although this infamous libel is quite as absurd

Black Diamonds Gathered in the Darkey Homes of the South (New York: Pudney & Russell, 1859), pp. 18-28.

and undeserving of contradiction as the famed Arrowsmith hoax, or any of the Sanguinary Crowbar style of negro-worship fictions, it deserves notice in one respect. There are a number of Yankee doughfaces in the South, who, before us, are the greatest admirers of the *peculiar institution,* and, to honey-fuggle us, even chime in with the abuse of their own section. There is danger in these men of disguised character, many of whom are doing business in the South. They are not to be trusted; and while, not satisfied with being tolerated among us, they impose on our confidence and hospitality by their professions, they take secret opportunities to gratify their real hatred of us, by tampering with the slaves, or by libelling the South under the shelter of anonymous letters published in the North. The man who would devise a safe opportunity to publish what he knew to be false and libellous of those whose good will he had won by another lie, might, with the same hope of impunity, venture on a grander revenge, and secretly conspire with the slave in a rebellion.

But it is not my purpose to trouble you with a dissertation on "the vexed question," or the social system of the South, or any of the political aspects of Slavery. I merely design to employ a few leisure hours in a series of unpretending sketches of the condition, habits, and peculiarities of the negro-slave. The field, you know, has furnished a number of books; and I am sure, my dear C., that you are too sensible of the large share of public attention *niggers* occupy in this country to slight them. Besides, I am thoroughly convinced that the negro portraits of the fiction writers are, most of them, mere caricatures, taking them all, from "Uncle Tom's Cabin," down to the latest reply thereto—"a book" from a Virginia authoress, in which the language put in the mouth of her leading character is a mixture of Irish idioms with the dialect of the Bowery. Who ever heard a Southern negro say, as the Virginia lady's sable hero does, "The tip-top of the morning to you, young ladies!" or "What's to pay now?" Nor will we find any of Mrs. Stowe's *Uncle Toms* in the South, at least so far as the religious portraiture goes. The negro, in his religion, is not a solemn old gentleman, reading his Bible in corners and praying in his closet: his piety is one of fits and starts, and lives on prayer-meetings, with its rounds of 'zortations, shoutings, and stolen sweets of baked pig.

You already know my opinion of the peculiarities of the negro's condition in the South, in the provision made for his comfort, and in the attachment between him and his master. The fact is, that, in wandering from my native soil to other parts of the world, I have seen slavery in many forms and aspects. We have all heard enough of the colliers and factory operatives of England, and the thirty thousand costermongers starving in the streets of London; as also of the serfs and crown-peasants of Russia, who are considered not even as chattels, but as part of the land, and who have their wives selected for them by their masters. I have seen the hideous slavery of Asia. I have seen the coolies of China "housed on the wild sea with wilder usages," or creeping with dejected faces into the suicide houses of Canton. I have seen the Siamese slave creeping in the presence of his master on all-fours —a human quadruped. It was indeed refreshing, after such sights, to get back to the Southern institution, which strikes one after so many years of absence, with a novelty that makes him appreciate more than ever the evidences of comfort and happiness on the plantations of the South.

The first unadulterated negro I had seen for a number of years (having been absent for the most of that time on a foreign soil), was on the railroad cars in Virginia. He looked like *home*. I could have embraced the old uncle, but was afraid the passengers, from such a demonstration, might mistake me for an abolitionist. I looked at him with my face aglow, and my eyelids touched with tears. How he reminded me of my home—of days gone by—that poetry of youth, "when I was a boy," and wandered with my sable playmates over the warm, wide hills of my sweet home, and along the branches, fishing in the shallow waters with a crooked pin! But no romancing with the past! So we continue our journey onward to "the State of railways and revolvers."

Arrived in Georgia, I find plenty of the real genuine *woolly-heads*, such as don't part their hair in the middle, like Mass'r Fremont. My first acquaintance is with Aunt Debby. I insist upon giving her a shake of the hand, which she prepares for by deprecatingly wiping her hand on her apron. Aunt Debby is an aged colored female of the very highest respectability, and, with her white apron, and her head mysteriously enveloped in the brightest of bandannas, she looks (to use one of her own rather obscure similes) "like a new pin." She is very fond of usurping the authority of her mistress below stairs, and has the habit of designating every one of her own color, not admitted to equality, as *"de nigger."* Aunt Debby is rather spoiled, if having things her own way means it. If at times her mistress is roused to dispute her authority, Aunt Debby is sure to resume the reins when quiet ensues. "Debby," cries her mistress, "what's all this noise in the kitchen—what are you whipping Lucy for?" "La, missis, I'se jest makin' her 'have herself. She too busy *walling* her eyes at me, and spilt the water on the steps." Among the children, Aunt Debby is a great character. She is, however, very partial; and her favorite is little Nina, whom she calls (from what remote analogy we are at a loss to conjecture) "her *jelly-pot*." I flatter myself that I am in her good graces. Her attention to me has been shown by a present of ground-peas, and accessions of fat lightwood to my fire in the morning.

The religious element is very strong in Aunt Debby's character, and her *repertoire* of pious minstrelsy is quite extensive. Her favorite hymn is in the following words, which are repeated over and over again:

> "Oh run, brother, run! Judgement day is comin'!
> Oh run, brother, run! Why don't you come along?
> The road so rugged, and the hill so high—
> And my Lord call me home,
> To walk the golden streets of my New Jerusalem."

Aunt Debby's religion is of that sort—always begging the Lord to take her up to glory, and professing the greatest anxiety to go *right now!* This religious enthusiasm, however, is not to be taken at its word.

You have doubtless heard the anecdote of Caesar, which is too good not to have been told more than once; though even if you have heard the story before, it will bear repetition for its moral. Now, Caesar one day had caught it, not from Brutus, but from

Betty—an allegorical coquette in the shape of a red cowhide. On retiring to the silence of his cabin at night, Caesar commenced to soliloquize, rubbing the part of his body where the castigation had been chiefly administered, and bewailing his fate with tragic desperation, in the third person. "Caesar," said he, "most done gone —don't want to live no·longer! Jist come, good Lord, swing low de chariot, and take dis chile away! Caesar ready to go—he *wants* to go!" An irreverent darkey outside, hearing these protestations, tapped at the door. "Who dar?" replied Caesar, in a low voice of suppressed alarm. "De angel of de Lord come for Caesar, 'cordin to request." The dread summons had indeed come, thought Caesar; but blowing out the light with a sudden whiff, he replied, in an unconcerned tone, *"De nigger don't live here."*

There is one other trait wanting to complete Aunt Debby's character. Though at an advanced age, she is very coquettish; and keeps a regular assault on a big lout of the name of Sam, whom she affects to despise as "jist 'de meanest nigger de Lord ever put breath in." I overheard some words between them last holiday. "I'se a white man to-day," says Sam, "and I'se not gwine to take any of your imperence, old ooman;" at the same time, taking the familiar liberty of poking his finger into her side like a brad-awl. "Get 'long, Sa-ten!" replied Aunt Debby, with a shove, but a smile at the same time, to his infernal majesty. And then they both fell to laughing for the space of half a minute, although I must confess, that I could not understand what they were laughing at.

Aunt Debby may serve you, my dear C., as a picture of the happy, contented, Southern slave. Some of your Northern politicians would represent the slaves of the South as sullen, gloomy, isolated from life—in fact, pictures of a living death. Believe me, nothing could be further from the truth. Like Aunt Debby, they have their little prides and passions, their amusements, their pleasantries, which constitute the same sum of happiness as in the lives of their masters.

The whipping-post and the slave mart are constantly paraded before the eyes of the poor, deluded fanatics of your section. Now I can assure you that the inhuman horrors of the slave auction-

block exist only in imagination. Many instances of humanity may
be observed there; and but seldom does the influence of the almighty
dollar appear to sway other and better considerations in the
breast of the slaveholder. The separation of families at the block
has come to be of very unfrequent occurrence, although the tempta-
tion is obvious to do so, as they generally sell much better when
the families are separated, and especially as the traders, who usually purchase for immediate realization, do not wish small children.
Indeed, there is a statute in this State (Georgia) forbidding the
sale of slave children of tender age away from their parents.

I attended a slave auction here the other day. The negroes were
called up in succession on the steps of the court-house, where the
crier stood. Naturally most of them appeared anxious as the bidding was going on, turning their eyes from one bidder to the other;
while the scene would be occasionally enlivened by some jest in
depreciation of the negro on the stand, which would be received
with especial merriment by his fellow negroes, who awaited their
turn, and looked on from a large wagon in which they were placed.
As I came up, a second-rate plantation hand of the name of Noah,
but whom the crier persisted in calling "Noey," was being offered,
it being an administrator's sale. Noey, on mounting the steps, had
assumed a most drooping aspect, hanging his head and affecting
the feebleness of old age. He had probably hoped to have avoided
a sale by a dodge, which is very common in such cases. But the
first bid—$1,000—startled him, and he looked eagerly to the quar-
ter whence it proceeded. "Never mind who he is, he has got the
money. Now, gentlemen, just go on; who will say fifty?" And so the
crier proceeds with his monotonous calling. "I aint worth all that,
mass'r; I aint much 'count no how," cries Noey energetically to the
first bidder. "Yes, you are, Noey—ah, $1,010, thank you, sir,"
replies the crier. The gentleman who makes this bid is recognized by
Noey as "Mass'r John," one of the heirs. $1,011, rejoins the first
bidder, and Noey throws a glance of infinite disdain at him for his
presumption in bidding against his master. But as the bidders call
over each other, Noey becomes more excited. "Drive on, Mass'r
John," he exclaims, laughing with excitement. The bidding is very
slow. Mass'r John evidently hesitates at the last call, $1,085, as too

large a price for the slave, though anxious to bid the poor fellow in; but Noey is shouting to him, amid the incitements of the crowd, to "Drive on;" and, after a pause, he says in a firm tone, *eleven hundred dollars*. The crier calls out the round numbers with a decided emphasis. He looks at the first bidder, who is evidently making up his mind whether to go higher, while Noey is regarding him, too, with a look of the keenest suspense. The man shakes his head at last, the hammer falls, and Noey, with an exulting whoop, dashes down the steps to his master.

Yours truly,   E. A. P.
To D. M. C., Esq., N. Y.

J. D. B. DeBOW (1820-1867)

THE INTEREST IN SLAVERY OF THE SOUTHERN NON-SLAVEHOLDER.

THE GREAT AUTHORITY OF James Dunwoody Brownson DeBow as a spokesman for Southern slavery derived from his familiarity with statistics, which he could quote for any purpose (he had served for a time as Superintendent of the Census), and from his position as editor of *DeBow's Review*, whose circulation was bigger than that of any other Southern magazine. The bustling port of New Orleans was the center of DeBow's universe, and from his editorial masthead he proclaimed repeatedly that Cotton was King.

By the late 1850s the South's concern with slavery was no longer to uphold the institution in debate, so much as to protect its own moral and intellectual solidarity against subversion. One of the system's perennial weaknesses had been the envy of the non-slaveholding classes for the planting gentry. The counterbalance was the benefits of caste that slavery guaranteed to white men throughout Southern society, which had been a regular theme of the system's defenders, but the publication of Hinton R. Helper's *Impending Crisis* in 1857 seemed to indicate that this side of the pro-slavery argument needed some fresh emphasis. The following essay by DeBow was one such effort.

. . . WHEN IN CHARGE of the national census office, several years since, I found that it had been stated by an abolition Senator from his seat, that the number of slaveholders at the South did not exceed 150,000. Convinced that it was a gross misrepresentation of the facts, I caused a careful examination of the returns to be made, which fixed the actual number at 347,255, and communicated the information, by note, to Senator Cass, who read it in the Senate. I first called attention to the fact that the number embraced slaveholding families, and that to arrive at the actual number of slaveholders, it would be necessary to multiply by the proportion of

"The Non-Slaveholders of the South," in DeBow and others, *The Interest in Slavery of the Southern Non-Slaveholder. The Right of Peaceful Secession. Slavery in the Bible.* (Charleston: Evans & Cogswell, 1860), pp. 3-5, 7-12.

persons, which the census showed to a family. When this was done, the number was swelled to about 2,000,000.

Since these results were made public, I have had reason to think, that the separation of the schedules of the slave and the free, was calculated to lead to omissions of the single properties, and that on this account it would be safe to put the number of families at 375,000, and the number of actual slaveholders at about two million and a quarter.

Assuming the published returns, however, to be correct, it will appear that one-half of the population of South Carolina, Mississippi, and Louisiana, excluding the cities, are slaveholders, and that one-third of the population of the entire South are similarly circumstanced. The average number of slaves is nine to each slave-holding family, and one-half of the whole number of such holders are in possession of less than five slaves.

It will thus appear that the slaveholders of the South, so far from constituting numerically an insignificant portion of its people, as has been malignantly alleged, make up an aggregate, greater in relative proportion than the holders of any other species of property whatever, in any part of the world; and that of no other property can it be said, with equal truthfulness, that it is an interest of the whole community. Whilst every other family in the States I have specially referred to, are slaveholders, but one family in every three and a half families in Maine, New Hampshire, Massachusetts and Connecticut, are holders of agricultural land; and, in European States, the proportion is almost indefinitely less, The proportion which the slaveholders of the South, bear to the entire population is greater than that of the owners of land or houses, agricultural stock, State, bank, or other corporation securities anywhere else. No political economist will deny this. Nor is that all. Even in the States which are among the largest slaveholding, South Carolina, Georgia and Tennessee, the land proprietors outnumber nearly two to one, in relative proportion, the owners of the same property in Maine, Massachusetts and Connecticut, and if the average number of slaves held by each family throughout the South be but nine, and if one-half of the whole number of slaveholders own under five slaves, it will be seen how preposterous is the allegation of our enemies, that the slaveholding class is an organized wealthy aristocracy. *The poor men of the South are the holders of one to five slaves, and it would be equally consistent with truth and justice, to say that they represent, in reality, its slaveholding interest.*

The fact being conceded that there is a very large class of persons in the slaveholding States, who have no direct ownership in slaves; it may be well asked, upon what principle a greater antagonism can be presumed between them and their fellow-citizens, than exists among the larger class of non-landholders in the free States and the landed interest there? If a conflict of interest exists in one instance, it does in the other, and if patriotism and public spirit are to be measured upon so low a standard, the social fabric at the North is in far greater danger of dissolution than it is here.

Though I protest against the false and degrading standard, to which Northern orators and statesmen have reduced the measure of patriotism, which is to be expected from a free and enlightened people, and in the name of the non-slaveholders of the South, fling back the insolent charge that they are only bound to their country by its "loaves and fishes," and would be found derelict in honor and principle and public virtue in proportion as they are needy in circumstances; I think it but easy to show that the interest of the poorest non-slaveholder among us, is to make common cause with, and die in the last trenches in defence of, the slave property of his more favored neighbor.

The non-slaveholders of the South may be classed as either such as desire and are incapable of purchasing slaves, or such as have the means to purchase and do not because of the absence of the motive, preferring to hire or employ cheaper white labor. A class conscientiously objecting to the ownership of slave-property, does not exist at the South, for all such scruples have long since been silenced by the profound and unanswerable arguments to which Yankee controversy has driven our statesmen, popular orators and clergy. Upon the sure testimony of God's Holy Book, and upon the principles of universal polity, they have defended and justified the institution. The exceptions which embrace recent importations into Virginia, and into some of the Southern cities from the free States of the

North, and some of the crazy, socialistic Germans in Texas, are too unimportant to affect the truth of the proposition. . . .

1. *The non-slaveholder of the South is assured that the remuneration afforded by his labor, over and above the expense of living, is larger than that which is afforded by the same labor in the free States.* To be convinced of this he has only to compare the value of labor in the Southern cities with those of the North, and to take note annually of the large number of laborers who are represented to be out of employment there, and who migrate to our shores, as well as to other sections. No white laborer in return has been forced to leave our midst or remain without employment. Such as have left, have immigrated from States where slavery was less productive. Those who come among us are enabled soon to retire to their homes with a handsome competency. The statement is nearly as true for the agricultural as for other interests, as the statistics will show.

The following table was recently compiled by Senator Johnson, of Tennessee, from information received in reply to a circular letter sent to the points indicated.

Daily wages in New Orleans, Charleston and Nashville:

Bricklayers.	Carpenters.	Laborers.
$2½ to 3½	$2¼ to 2¾	$1 to 1½.

Daily wages in Chicago, Pittsburgh and Lowell, Mass.:

Bricklayers.	Carpenters.	Laborers.
$1½ to $2	$1½ to 1¾	75c to $1.

The rates of board weekly for laborers as given in the census of 1850, were in Louisiana $2 70, South Carolina $1 75, Tennessee $1 32, in Illinois $1 49, Pennsylvania $1 72, Massachusetts $2 12. The wages of the agricultural classes as given in Parliamentary reports are in France $20 to $30 per annum with board. In Italy $12 to $20 per annum. In the United States agricultural labor is highest in the Southwest, and lowest in the Northwest, the South and North differing very little, by the official returns.

2. *The non-slaveholders, as a class, are not reduced by the necessity of our condition, as is the case in the free States, to find employment in crowded cities and come into competition in close and*

*sickly workshops and factories, with remorseless and untiring ma-
chinery.* They have but to compare their condition in this particular
with the mining and manufacturing operatives of the North and
Europe, to be thankful that God has reserved them for a better fate.
Tender women, aged men, delicate children, toil and labor there
from early dawn until after candle light, from one year to another,
for a miserable pittance, scarcely above the starvation point and
without hope of amelioration. The records of British free labor have
long exhibited this and those of our own manufacturing States are
rapidly reaching it and would have reached it long-ago, but for the
excessive bounties which in the way of tariffs have been paid to it,
without an equivalent by the slaveholding and non-slaveholding
laborer of the South. Let this tariff cease to be paid for a single year
and the truth of what is stated will be abundantly shown.

3. *The non-slaveholder is not subjected to that competition with
foreign pauper labor, which has degraded the free labor of the North
and demoralized it to an extent which perhaps can never be estimated.* From whatever cause, it has happened, whether from climate, the nature of our products or of our labor, the South has been
enabled to maintain a more homogeneous population and show a less
admixture of races than the North. This the statistics show.

RATIO OF FOREIGN TO NATIVE POPULATION.

Eastern States.............................12.65 in every 100
Middle States..............................19.84 " "
Southern States............................1.86 " "
South-western States.......................5.34 " "
North-western States.......................12.75 " "

Our people partake of the true American character, and are
mainly the descendants of those who fought the battles of the
Revolution, and who understand and appreciate the nature and
inestimable value of the liberty which it brought. Adhering to the
simple truths of the Gospel and the faith of their fathers, they have
not run hither and thither in search of all the absurd and degrading
isms which have sprung up in the rank soil of infidelity. They are
not Mormons or Spiritualists, they are not Owenites, Fourierites,
Agrarians, Socialists, Free-lovers or Millerites. They are not for

breaking down all the forms of society and of religion and re-constructing them; but prefer law, order and existing institutions to the chaos which radicalism involves. The competition between native and foreign labor in the Northern States, has already begotten rivalry and heart-burning, and riots; and lead to the formation of political parties there which have been marked by a degree of hostility and proscription to which the present age has not afforded another parallel. At the South we have known none of this, except in two or three of the larger cities, where the relations of slavery and freedom scarcely exist at all. The foreigners that are among us at the South are of a select class, and from education and example approximate very nearly to the native standard.

4. *The non-slaveholder of the South preserves the status of the white man, and is not regarded as an inferior or a dependent.* He is not told that the Declaration of Independence, when it says that all men are born free and equal, refers to the negro equally with himself. It is not proposed to him that the free negro's vote shall weigh equally with his own at the ballot-box, and that the little children of both colors shall be mixed in the classes and benches of the school-house, and embrace each other filially in its outside sports. It never occurs to him, that a white man could be degraded enough to boast in a public assembly, as was recently done in New York, of having actually slept with a negro. And his patriotic ire would crush with a blow the free negro who would dare, in his presence, as is done in the free States, to characterize the father of the country as a "scoundrel." No white man at the South serves another as a body servant, to clean his boots, wait on his table, and perform the menial services of his household. His blood revolts against this, and his necessities never drive him to it. He is a companion and an equal. When in the employ of the slaveholder, or in intercourse with him, he enters his hall, and has a seat at his table. If a distinction exists, it is only that which education and refinement may give, and this is so courteously exhibited as scarcely to strike attention. The poor white laborer at the North is at the bottom of the social ladder, whilst his brother here has ascended several steps and can look down upon those who are beneath him, at an infinite remove.

5. *The non-slaveholder knows that as soon as his savings will admit, he can become a slaveholder, and thus relieve his wife from the necessities of the kitchen and the laundry, and his children from the labors of the field.* This, with ordinary frugality, can, in general, be accomplished in a few years, and is a process continually going on. Perhaps twice the number of poor men at the South own a slave to what owned a slave ten years ago. The universal disposition is to purchase. It is the first use for savings, and the negro purchased is the last possession to be parted with. If a woman, her children become heir-looms and make the nucleus of an estate. It is within my knowledge, that a plantation of fifty or sixty persons has been established, from the descendants of a single female, in the course of the lifetime of the original purchaser.

6. *The large slaveholders and proprietors of the South begin life in great part as non-slaveholders.* It is the nature of property to change hands. Luxury, liberality, extravagance, depreciated land, low prices, debt, distribution among children, are continually breaking up estates. All over the new States of the South-west enormous estates are in the hands of men who began life as overseers or city clerks, traders or merchants. Often the overseer marries the widow. Cheap lands, abundant harvests, high prices, give the poor man soon a negro. His ten bales of cotton bring him another, a second crop increases his purchases, and so he goes on opening land and adding labor until in a few years his draft for $20,000 upon his merchant becomes a very marketable commodity.

7. *But should such fortune not be in reserve for the non-slaveholder, he will understand that by honesty and industry it may be realized to his children.* More than one generation of poverty in a family is scarcely to be expected at the South, and is against the general experience. It is more unusual here for poverty than wealth to be preserved through several generations in the same family.

8. *The sons of the non-slaveholder are and have always been among the leading and ruling spirits of the South; in industry as well as in politics.* Every man's experience in his own neighborhood will evince this. He has but to task his memory. In this class are the McDuffies, Langdon Cheves, Andrew Jacksons, Henry Clays, and

Rusks, of the past; the Hammonds, Yanceys, Orrs, Memmingers, Benaminjs, Stephens, Soulés, Browns of Mississippi, Simms, Porters, Magraths, Aikens, Maunsel Whites, and an innumerable host of the present; and what is to be noted, these men have not been made demagogues for that reason, as in other quarters, but are among the most conservative among us. Nowhere else in the world have intelligence and virtue disconnected from ancestral estates, the same opportunities for advancement, and nowhere else is their triumph more speedy and signal.

9. *Without the institution of slavery, the great staple products of the South would cease to be grown, and the immense annual results, which are distributed among every class of the community, and which give life to every branch of industry, would cease.* The world furnishes no instances of these products being grown upon a large scale by free labor. The English now acknowledge their failure in the East Indies. Brazil, whose slave population nearly equals our own, is the only South American State which has prospered. Cuba, by her slave labor, showers wealth upon old Spain, whilst the British West India Colonies have now ceased to be a source of revenue, and from opulence have been, by emancipation, reduced to beggary. St. Domingo shared the same fate, and the poor whites have been massacred equally with the rich. . . .

10. *If emancipation be brought about as will undoubtedly be the case, unless the encroachments of the fanatical majorities of the North are resisted now the slaveholders, in the main, will escape the degrading equality which must result, by emigration, for which they would have the means, by disposing of their personal chattels: whilst the non-slaveholders, without these resources, would be compelled to remain and endure the degradation.* This is a startling consideration. In Northern communities, where the free negro is one in a hundred of the total population, he is recognized and acknowledged often as a pest, and in many cases even his presence is prohibited by law. What would be the case in many of our States, where every other inhabitant is a negro, or in many of our communities, as for example the parishes around and about Charleston, and in the vicinity of New Orleans where there are from twenty to one

hundred negroes to each white inhabitant? Low as would this class of people sink by emancipation in idleness, superstition and vice, the white man compelled to live among them, would by the power exerted over him, sink even lower, unless as is to be supposed he would prefer to suffer death instead. . . .

SUGGESTIONS FOR FURTHER READING,

And

ACKNOWLEDGMENTS.

TWO MAJOR COLLECTIONS OF pro-slavery writing were brought out by Southern publishers in the decade preceding the Civil War: *The Pro-Slavery Argument; as Maintained by . . . Chancellor Harper, Governor Hammond, Dr. Simms, and Professor Dew* (Charleston: Walker, Richards & Co., 1852); and E. N. Elliott, ed., *Cotton is King, and Pro-Slavery Arguments: Comprising the Writings of Hammond, Harper, Christy, Stringfellow, Hodge, Bledsoe, and Cartwright . . .* (Augusta: Pritchard, Abbott & Loomis, 1860). Though these compendiums do not include all the best work of the period, the selections they do include are reprinted in full.

Works which analyze the pro-slavery effort as an intellectual movement are William Sumner Jenkins, *Pro-Slavery Thought in the Old South* (Chapel Hill: University of North Carolina Press, 1935), which is very useful in classifying the various forms which the argument took; Clement Eaton, *Freedom of Thought in the Old South* (Durham: Duke University Press, 1940), an account of what the defense of slavery did to Southern intellectual life in general; Louis Hartz, *The Liberal Tradition in America* (New York: Harcourt, Brace, 1955), pp. 145-200, an analysis of how slavery influenced the South's political thought; and Joseph Dorfman, *The Economic Mind in American Civilization, 1606-1865* (New York: The Viking Press, 1946), II, 881-956, which deals with those pro-slavery intellectuals whose work had implications for economic thought. William Stanton, *The Leopard's Spots: Scientific Attitudes Toward Race in America, 1815-59* (Chicago: University of Chicago Press, 1960), deals tangentially with one aspect of the pro-slavery argument. (For the most recent scientific thought, see Carleton S. Coon, "New Findings on the Origin of Races," *Harper's Magazine*, December 1962, pp. 66-74.) William R. Taylor, *Cavalier and Yankee: The Old South and American National Character* (George Braziller, 1961), is an imaginative reconstruction of the aristocratic myth which helped the South picture slavery to itself as a plausible and natural institution. Stanley Elkins, *Slavery, A Problem in American Institutional and Intellectual Life* (University of Chicago Press, 1959), esp. pp. 206-222, considers the social psychology not only of slavery itself but also of slavery's intellectual defenders.

Shorter essays which are of particular value in understanding the pro-slavery movement are: Richard Hofstadter, "John C. Calhoun: Marx of the Master Class," in *The American Political Tradition* (New York: A. A. Knopf, 1948), pp. 67-91; C. Vann Woodward, "George Fitzhugh, *Sui Generis*," in George Fitzhugh, *Cannibals All! Or, Slaves Without Masters,* ed. C. V. Woodward (Cambridge: Harvard University Press, 1960), vii-xxxix; Stanley Elkins, "The Right to Be a Slave," *Commentary,* XXX (Nov. 1960), 450-452; Wilfred Carsel, "The Slaveholders' Indictment of Northern Wage Slavery," *Journal of Southern History,* VI (Nov. 1940), 504-520; and Ralph E. Morrow, "The Proslavery Argument Revisited," *Mississippi Valley Historical Review,* XLVII (June 1961), 79-93.

Material in book or article form dealing more specifically with individual writers includes: Harvey Wish, *George Fitzhugh, Propagandist of the Old South* (Baton Rouge: Louisiana State University Press, 1943); see also Professor Wish's introductory essay in H. Wish, ed., *Ante-Bellum: Writings of George Fitzhugh and Hinton Rowan Helper on Slavery* (New York: Capricorn Books, 1960); Edmund Wilson, "William J. Grayson" and "George Fitzhugh," in *Patriotic Gore: Studies in the Literature of the Civil War* (New York: Oxford University Press, 1962), pp. 336-364; Lowell Harrison, "Thomas Roderick Dew: Philosopher of the Old South," *Virginia Magazine of History and Biography,* LVII (October 1949), 390-404; Kenneth Stampp, "An Analysis of Dew's *Review of the Debates in the Virginia Legislature*," *Journal of Negro History,* XXVII (October 1942), 380-387; Harvey Wish, "George Frederick Holmes and Southern Periodical Literature of the Mid-Nineteenth Century," *Journal of Southern History,* VII (August 1941), 343-356; H. Wish, "George Frederick Holmes and the Genesis of American Sociology," *American Journal of Sociology,* XLVI (March 1941), 698-707; Avery O. Craven, *Edmund Ruffin, Southerner: A Study in Secession* (New York: D. Appleton, 1932); and Otis C. Skipper, *J. D. B. DeBow, Magazinist of the Old South* (Athens: University of Georgia Press, 1958). Most of the writers whose work has been included in the present collection are represented by biographical sketches in Allen Johnson and Dumas Malone, eds., *Dictionary of American Biography* (New York: Scribner's, 1930—).

For criticisms and suggestions on the preparation of this volume, es-pecially the Introductory Essay, I am indebted to four of my friends, Kingsley Ervin of Horace Mann School, Robert Cross of Columbia, Stanley Elkins of Smith, and C. Vann Woodward of Yale. In the locating and ar-ranging of the documents, the hours of assistance given me by Miss Mary-Jo Kline of Elmira, New York, are deeply appreciated.

The text of this book is set in Modern # 21, a Linotype face.
The book was designed by Bob Melson, in the manner of books
published in America *circa* 1850.

Printed in the USA
CPSIA information can be obtained
at www.ICGtesting.com
LVHW020617150124
768656LV00006BB/459